"Everyone says you've got to get ready financially. No, no, you've got to get ready psychologically."

--Lee Iacocca

Life After Work:

Redefining Retirement

A step-by-step guide to balancing your life and achieving bliss in the Wisdom Years

ISBN-13 978-1-60145-125-5
ISBN-10 1-60145-125-3

Printed in the United States of America.

Booklocker.com, Inc.
2007

Life After Work

Redefining Retirement

A step-by-step guide to balancing your life and

achieving bliss in the Wisdom Years

BY DOUGLAS S. FLETCHER

TABLE OF CONTENTS

INTRODUCTION

The idea of retiring at a certain age and transitioning into full-time leisure is changing. Retirement was once the short time between the end of a person's productivity and death, just three years given the average life expectancy in the 1950s. Today we are living longer and retiring earlier, allowing us twenty-five or more years to pursue lifelong goals and passions. Rather than fading into the sunset, we have time to rediscover our personal uniqueness, deepen relationships, and question the mysteries of life. Yes, there is life after work and in this book, we redefine retirement. Welcome to the Wisdom Years.

Whether you are planning to retire, newly retired, long retired, or wishing you never retired, this book offers insights into the retirement process. You will learn the phases of retirement and transitions required to overcome career losses. You will discover how past beliefs influence present behavior patterns, perhaps limiting your personal growth. From studies of other retirees, you will explore happiness and how to take significant steps in your journey toward the Wisdom Years—where you search for the meaning and purpose of life.

The book includes descriptions of public figures who encountered hard times transitioning to retirement. This group includes professional athletes, corporate executives, media stars, political figures, and successful entrepreneurs. They are at most psychological risk because of their larger-than-life images. As average retirees, we can relate to their journeys and learn from their experiences.

Today's retirees are a varied group. Some are self-employed or professionals, such as doctors, lawyers, and teachers, who want to defer retirement and work as long as possible. Others are at the opposite end of the continuum, counting the days until they are free from having to earn a living. They cannot wait to do all the things they have always dreamed, to take trips, pursue hobbies, and finish projects.

Regardless of where you fall on the continuum, you will face the same issues—the losses and transitions synonymous with retirement. After reading this book you will realize: retirement offers all kinds of possibilities. You are free to do many things you desire. You are empowered. What you make of the rest of your life is up to you.

Together, let's start the journey to the Wisdom Years.

CHAPTER ONE: THE FOUR PHASES OF RETIREMENT

The first few years after Charles retired were great. He did all the things he didn't have time to do while working. He added a room to his house, cycled with his friends, and volunteered with Habitat for Humanity. Then came the search for something important to do with his life. At first, it was about buying a boat to restore and sail with his wife. He was looking for a wooden boat with a soul so he could bring it back to its original beauty. He discovered boats were endless money pits, especially wooden boats. Giving up on the idea, Charles was at a dead end—discouraged, and frustrated. To find purpose and fulfillment, he began to identify his gifts and passions. This led him on a different path—to writing a book—wherein he experienced a renewed zest for life. Charles had journeyed into the Wisdom Years.

We use the term Wisdom Years to describe the retirement stage where we begin to search for the meaning and purpose of life. It does not happen overnight. Charles's transition followed a typical pattern: first, the honeymoon stage where there was time to do everything and anything. Then came the period of disappointment and loss. Realizing he could not recapture the past, Charles began searching for something more. Little did he realize he was looking for himself.

PHASE ONE: THE HONEYMOON

For three or five years, or however long it takes to fulfill lifelong dreams, initially retirement is about activities. It marks a switch from on-the-job tasks to an unstructured daily routine. We worked so hard, we deserve this time to travel, fix up the house, spend more time with the grandchildren, or visit old friends. Thus, it often results in "The Activity Trap"—excessive travel, workouts, golf, managing stock portfolios, visiting grandkids, etc.

Then apprehensions begin to creep in. Though hard to identify at first, these are feelings of loss. Having suffered the typical losses in midlife, we might assume we would understand the losses of these years. Not so. The retirement experience is different. There is finality to the next third of life that can lead to anxiety—sinking into the "abyss of insignificance" because something is missing.

PHASE TWO: LOSS AND DENIAL

If retirement is mythologized as a time of idyllic pleasure, then many retirees are in for a surprise. Few people enter retirement knowing how to cope with the five unavoidable losses (discussed in the next chapter): structure, identity, relationships, purpose, and power.

Loss and denial are two conflicting feelings in retirement resulting from the attempt to preserve what was—to hold on to the past. When we glimpse the expensive suits and shoes we will never wear again, even our closets remind us we are not who we used to be. We want to feel satisfaction from our personal contacts, our hobbies, and our daily routine. Being valued and feeling productive make us feel good. Stripped of this fundamental feeling, we may compensate by succumbing to the activity trap, by gambling, exercising excessively, drinking, or overeating. Or we may go into denial.

Take Dave for example. For the longest time it was hard for Dave to even say the "R" word. Even after retiring, he remained active in the accounting business and spent time fly-fishing. Truth be told, he did not consider himself retired. As he began to work less and have more free time, he developed a subtle fear. He resisted the stereotypical "old" people activities, like signing up for a cruise, attending a senior center event, or accepting an AARP offer. Consenting to any of these meant he was on his way to a nursing home, like his parents. With his resistance to the "R" word, aging, and the loss of full-time work, Dave was in denial.

Given the lack of psychological planning, it is not surprising that few want to talk about what is ahead. When brought up in social gatherings, the word retirement often produces a deadening silence. To preserve self-image, denial makes sense and our actions feel right. To lose self-image is to lose identity and this is a frightening prospect.

Refusing to talk about it is hardly the answer. The longer we put off facing retirement issues, the more emotional damage we risk. We may become critical and judgmental. We may feel people are picking on us. In extreme cases, we may see ourselves as victims. Since what we do looks right to us, we may begin to blame people around us for our frustrations and project our pain onto others, often our loved ones. A directionless, unhappy, and critical person is a candidate for mild depression.

Don't kid yourself—no one escapes the feelings of loss in the retirement years. Any time you stop full-time work, even if part-time work is in your future, you experience the five career losses: structure, identity, relationships, purpose, and power discussed in the next chapter. But the pain of loss propels us to take action and experiment.

PHASE THREE: EXPERIMENTING

Retirement offers an enormous opportunity to change ourselves. While we are still relatively young with money, energy, and health, each of us can look at the world and say, "Okay, what do I do next?" By experimenting, we redefine passions and ensure gratifying and fulfilling lives. The question is: How do I make a contribution that elevates the daily routine above mere mediocrity?

When asked, "Why do anything? Why not retire?" Lee Iacocca, who initially flunked his early retirement, responded, "My kids ask me that all the time 'What the hell are you doing investing in a dot-com startup?' I've played enough golf. The world is changing and I want to keep talking to young people and see all these wonderful new markets and inventions. I already own a big electric bike business, but with

Online Asset Exchange I realize I can learn a lot and, through my fifty tough years in business, I can help them."

For those without venture capital to invest, it is a matter of trying something, finding out if it feels right, and settling into that role or trying something else. The high stakes we faced in our career years are not a factor now. There is no corporate ladder to climb. However, many people want to contribute and try to find roles compatible with their professional experiences.

Pursue as many choices as possible. Time is not an issue and we need not make choices quickly. Endeavors we once thought as uninviting, may turn out to be interesting opportunities. The key is not to do what everyone else does. Volunteering is not for everyone and many will never sit on company boards. What is gratifying for some, may well turn off others. As one leader put it, "Retirement often begins with false starts. While momentarily frustrating, this is not a permanent obstacle. Experimenting is a good thing. It is wise to look at the transition as realistically as possible."

Choose based on interests and full-hearted participation. The activity is not a time-filling diversion or a time-restricted endeavor like a full-time career. Our choices need to be governed by what is personally creative and socially significant. Not to say these endeavors can't be financially profitable. Experiment with many intriguing opportunities. Whatever you can do or dream, do it.

PHASE FOUR: THE RETIREMENT WIN

Retirement provides the time to ponder important life questions. But it is not easy.

Consider Bill's story, for example. Believing he had it all together, Bill still asked, "Is this all I have to look forward to? Can I stand to be in this place for another twenty years and become bitter? Am I fated to reflect on the past, without any anticipation of the future? Is there no value in who I am now, with my career successes and experience? Where will I put my energy?"

We don't start our lives questioning our purpose. We may ponder the question in college, but with a job, a mortgage, and kids, we push the question away. Only when we lose identity do we question purpose.

Stripped of position, authority, perks, an admiring staff, and the trappings of successful careers, we ponder what is important. After years of finding what works (and what doesn't), we back into the question of who we are and what is gratifying. The discovery of satisfaction in any endeavor is essential and fulfills a basic human longing. As a result of such reflection, a purposeless existence finds resolution.

The *Harvard Business Review* article, "Reawakening Your Passion for Work" reports that we are driven by a passion to lead, to serve the customer, and to support a cause or a product. If passion fades, we begin to question the value of our work. The once rewarding job becomes less important. We may confuse the achievement of high goals with satisfaction until we become bored. Or we may be nagged that we're not who we want to be. Instead of changing reality, we surrender to the organizational routine and then ask why we have no joy. Conditioned by an enduring work ethic, is it any wonder we do not have the skills to tackle the search for meaning in our post-career lives?

The subsequent chapter discusses the important transitions needed for the retirement win—how to embrace the present and develop structure, identity, relationships, purpose, and power in retirement. Each of us has the ability to create a future, which satisfies every aspect of our lives, our unique talents, relationships, health, and the very nature of our humanity.

PONDER THIS

Before leaving this chapter, ask yourself these questions:

- What stage of retirement am I in currently?
- What do I want in the last third of my life? (Who do I want to become?)
- How will I measure my success?

CHAPTER TWO: THE FIVE CAREER LOSSES

Andrew eyed the beautiful suits and spiffy ties as he walked through the men's department of his favorite store. He used to like to dress up for work and took pride in how he looked. For a moment, his knee-jerk reaction was to buy a couple of ties and a dress shirt or two. But he was hit with a realization—he had more ties and dress shirts than he would ever wear again. He was lucky to dress up once a month for a special occasion. Probably, he'd never need to buy another dress shirt or tie for the rest of his life. He let out a long sigh as the thought hit him in his solar plexus.

Like Andrew, you may find the changes in life after full-time work come as a shock. When you retire, your attire, your identity, and your self-image change as you walk out of your business for the last time. Work shores up identity, anchors the private and social self, and defines that self to the world. How will you deal with the losses you will experience in your post-career years as a result of not working?

Career losses fall into five categories: structure, identity, relationships, purpose, and power. As you read about the five losses, be honest with yourself: Which losses sting? What might you substitute for each loss? Where are the gaps?

STRUCTURE

For most of us, life has revolved around structure imposed by others. Schools provide early structure and military service imposes an even more intense structure. Business hours dictate the time we spend at work. Days are filled with weekly, monthly, and quarterly meetings scheduled on an annual calendar. Everything is planned so no time is wasted. Schedules are jam-packed with work and social commitments.

Not so in retirement. After the novelty of free time wears off and the long-overdue projects are behind us, there are an overwhelming number of unstructured blank days, months, and years ahead. Because feelings of fruitlessness can be overwhelming, it is a challenge to deal with this empty landscape.

Structure includes a place to go, routines, goals, meetings, conventions, a culture. At work, we had a destination, a place we were expected to be, even on the road or visiting clients. Without a designated space, we may choose the gym, the local coffee shop, or the club. If the home becomes the primary social space, we may find diversions like the TV, the refrigerator, or a disgruntled partner lead to depressing outcomes. Spouses often insist their newly retired partners rent office space because they need some place to go.

Take the boys, for example. They gather each morning and stand around talking at Dad's Donuts or they sit around the big circular table at the yacht club for Thursday lunch. Each is a tight knit group of retirees. Different from the weekly foursome of golf, these gatherings offer light conversation and support. Such rituals provide structure and the much-needed social interaction since past work associates may move away or develop other friendships.

We must move from an outer-directed to a self-directed structure. It is up to each of us to find a routine and to create a discipline that puts us in healthy social settings where we are free to use our unique creative abilities.

IDENTITY

Who am I? In our careers, we had roles and responsibilities and job descriptions defining us. We managed our careers through these roles, but it was more about the role than who we were. Left with nothing to do or manage, we don't have anything else. We have lost social identity.

Take Pauline for example. She was president of a successful corporation, a genuine leader among her peers. She had transformed her organization and rallied people behind corporate and philanthropic causes. Listed among the top fifty women entrepreneurs, she enjoyed a competitive salary. Upon retirement, her visibility waned. No one returned her calls. She soon realized it was the office that caused people to respond. So Pauline traded in her Blackberry for a new computer and started blogging and connecting with others via e-mail. Online, she found a whole new way of interacting with people she'd never even met, thus rebuilding her identity.

Identity includes the job, position, status, and professional accomplishments. Often, identity is tied to earning power. We compare our earnings to others as a measure of success. Like in Monopoly, whoever has the most wins. Although we may have satisfactory pensions, we suffer a blow when we no longer receive our salaries.

In the Wisdom Years, we transition from social identity to personal identity. If loss of earning power is one blow to identity, aging is the other. We look in the mirror and do not recognize ourselves. Who is this older person staring back? For many, identity is tied to youthfulness. We took for granted the stamina and sharp senses of youth. Thriving on the pace of whirlwind meetings, air travel, and entertaining, we were praised for amazing stamina. One by one, these abilities wane and we replace them by rebuilding an identity steeped in the present.

RELATIONSHIPS

During the career years, our relationships included work friends, the team, associates, the sum resulting in feeling useful. In retirement, many of us feel an unexplainable loneliness, even though we may continue to have active social lives. We may not miss the people per se, but the bond of purposefulness—working toward common goals and solving problems with others. When we shared the ups and downs, the business lunches, the conventions, and the successes of winning, connections formed naturally.

Retirement marks the loss of many friends. Most business friendships are based on mutual advantage—what an individual wants from the other person. We enjoy the business benefit we gain from the contact. Although some friendships blossom to include other activities, such as golf, business is the underlying connection. When a business reason no longer cements the bond, the friendship fades and it becomes obvious that many were not friends at all. Some friends move away and others, for lack of any common bond, fade away. After forty years of a built-in support group, this loss can come as a shock.

How do we cope with such loss? If we are unable to recreate such important bonds, we may resign ourselves to the realization: we will never again feel the collective energy and comradery of being in business.

Even relationships with our spouses change. Our inability to downshift and treat our spouses differently results in feelings of being misunderstood and unappreciated. Take Lois for example. She believed her husband would be different after retirement and became angry when her needs were not understood. Just when she thought she had a friend, she found a husband who still craved the limelight and needed to be nurtured. She felt drained, having to give so much. She expressed her anger by criticizing him and pointing out every time he was wrong, Subconsciously, he may have added to the conflict by trying to regain a feeling of being in control. This blue funk of the transition did not end until they developed a renewed purpose in life.

We must transition from results-oriented to heartfelt connections. The ability to make heartfelt connections independent of a working environment is a new skill for many. The emotional element of a relationship is the value.

PURPOSE

At work we had common goals and shared decision-making, leading to results and winning. For most of us, work was an expression of uniqueness and an opportunity to translate talents into creative, valuable products. This made us feel good. We felt exhilaration from the pace of making decisions and getting results. We were viewed as critical contributors in an organization. People waited for our decisions and recognition came with the territory.

When working full time, we had common goals with our spouses—raise the kids, build careers, get established in the community, create social identity, and secure financial freedom. In retirement, goals may conflict.

Consider Tom and Sara's story. Tom doesn't feel in sync with his wife. Sara wants to visit her grandchildren; he doesn't feel the need. She wants to eat out; he says it costs too much. She needs to stay in touch with the family by phone; her spending in general, and the phone bill in particular, outrage him. Even with a comfortable retirement income, he objects to paying for a housekeeper. Having managed a business with a budget, Tom takes the same approach with the household expenses. Used to flexible spending, Sara finds Tom's money management is driving her nuts.

Tom and Sara are going in opposite directions—they have different agendas. He is exerting control over expenses, even though he has a comfortable nest egg. Perhaps he is trying to conserve cash now that his earning power is fixed.

Regardless, the underlying problem has more to do with unclear goals then finances. Without mutual goals, he finds the relationship with his wife has deteriorated. Tom has reached a significant point: he must transition from business success to being a significant other.

POWER

Title, budget responsibility, technical expertise, number of direct reports, making important decisions, office size, and proximity to the big boss, all convey power of position. People with position power initiate action just by picking up the phone.

But position power creates a false sense of importance. When we leave our full-time careers, we encounter problems with attitudes, expectations, and how people respond to us.

As Howard Shank says in his book, *Managing Retirement*, "The problem has a name. The name is importance." Take away the power vested in the position and an individual is stripped of the feeling of being important. The solution is not to find important work, but to find something important to replace the lost position power.

When we retire, we no longer have position power. If we try to do something in the volunteer or philanthropic world and revert to our old management skills, we anger people. We cannot use the power of who we used to be.

We typically want to know we are in control. Making decisions brings the exhilaration of being in control. The loss of this elixir can cause severe anxiety. Lack of importance and less control results in frustration and humiliation.

Spouses complain household management comes under scrutiny when husbands face a control void and shift into a Mr. Fix-It mode.

Consider Ian's story. He was a former division manager, overseeing several production facilities. Having no productive activities upon retirement, he began applying the same rigid quality control standards of work to his home. His spouse resisted, politely ignoring his suggestions. She felt controlled and that her judgment was in question. The final straw was when he completely reorganized the pantry. He was excited at how much room he created and how neat everything looked. Ian was dismayed at his spouse's anger. He thought she would be pleased with his effort.

The boundless energy to control and solve problems is not needed at home. The spouse has done quite well for many years—thank you very much! Ian's behavior is understandable—he wants to feel productive and useful. However, pulling rank and attempting homemaker decisions is sure to backfire.

Losing position power comes at an age when other losses increase. In *Aging Well,* Dr. Andrew Weil suggests that, "The older you get, the more likely you are to experience loss—loss of parents, of family, of friends, of mates, of companion animals, of independence, of body functions, even body parts. Any loss can remind you of all losses, plunging you into grief and despair." Yet we have a choice as to how we interpret our losses—and our beliefs about how things should be.

The loss of control haunts us until we transition from position power to personal power. Personal power begins with the recognition that we can use our talents in a variety of ways—to do nothing beyond pleasing ourselves—to play golf, or to take an inner journey, discovering our spiritual essence. The authentic self is hidden, but there. Each of us has the power to make this decision. We have a third of life left—the best part—absolutely the best part.

PONDER THIS

Before leaving this chapter, ask yourself these questions:

- Which aspect of my career (structure, identity, relationships, purpose, power) did I enjoy the most and why?
- Which career aspect might I have the most difficulty replacing: structure, identity, relationships, purpose, power?
- How might I go about replacing that career loss?

CHAPTER THREE: THE BIG WINNERS, THE BIG LOSERS

"I flunked retirement," Lee Iacocca said of his three years after leaving as Chrysler's CEO. "I wasn't ready for it. Most people aren't, especially CEOs. Your life is so structured that you really become insulated. When you're a CEO, you never rub shoulders with people. When I flew corporate, I was alone most of the time. If there was a guy with me, he wanted to talk business. If a limo picked me up, I got to know the back of the driver's head. It was worse at Ford. They really treated you like a king, because Henry Ford II wanted it that way."

Iacocca talked about flunking retirement in an exclusive *Fortune* magazine interview. He says those retirement years were more stressful than his forty-seven years in the auto business. He is one of our poster boys, a highly recognized figure who depicts what is likely to happen.

Here is another example. He was a visionary, a successful industry executive, consultant, fund-raiser, and organizer of many civic causes. He had made significant contributions to business and nonprofit causes. Throughout his career, his wife supported him unselfishly behind the scenes. When there was finally time for them as a couple, he was unable to be there for her. He didn't give enough thought to his retirement and underestimated its effect on their marriage. As a patient in the nursing home, he was unable to relate to others; the nursing staff didn't want to hear of his accomplishments. So he took pride in not talking. He died angry, critical, and disillusioned—feeling insignificant and melancholy. He never separated who he was from what he did.

Who was this guy? He was my dad.

My dad's retirement represents the classic pattern: all work and no play makes for a sad retired person. Unable to relate to his family, to transition out of the spotlight, and to envision the opportunities of the Wisdom Years, he felt like he had been dropped into an abyss of insignificance.

Those who have had highly *structured careers* are at risk of failing retirement. Success is not the measure. The postal worker, the government employee, the politician, the cop—even CEOs and US presidents have sunk into an abyss in their attempts to manage the blank landscape of their post-career years. They have no clue how to shift from what they do to who they are.

RETIREMENT: AT RISK FOR THE ABYSS

Jeffery A. Sonnenfeld describes the often jarring shift into retirement "a plunge into the abyss of insignificance." Author of *The Hero's Farewell: What Happens When CEOs Retire*, Sonnenfeld observes that chief executives are at risk for the abyss when a lifetime of relation building dissolves before their eyes. We have broadened the label to include all professionals and managers in highly structured careers, small business owners, and people in positions garnering social status, such as judges, doctors, lawyers, and professional athletes.

REDEFINING RETIREMENT

Retirement was once defined as the short time between the end of one's productivity and death. Today, we are living longer and retiring earlier. In the 1950s, the average life expectancy was sixty-eight; in 2000 expectancy increased to seventy-six. For many of us, it will be more like eighty-six. Because of the baby boomer generation, the size and strength of the older population will increase. By the year 2030, the over-sixty-five population will number seventy million and comprise twenty-five percent of the total adult population.

Pre-retirement studies show that many middle-level respondents want to explore interests they never had the time to pursue. This is clear evidence that retirement is no longer about fading into the sunset. On the contrary, it is about rediscovering personal uniqueness, deepening relationships, and questioning the mysteries of life.

THERE ARE NO RULES

There are few guidelines for shifting gears and gliding into this stage of life's journey. We spent twenty-five years acquiring the tools, education, and beliefs about how to live—indoctrinated by our parents, teachers, the community, and the society. Then we spent another forty years performing at work.

During forty years of work, we had specific rules for competing in the marketplace, making a living, and saving for retirement. In the classic 1950s book, *The Organization Man*, William Whyte defined the underpinning of America's work ethic. He described able-bodied workers entering retirement as "the ones who have left home spiritually as well as physically to take the vows of organization life. From their ranks are coming most of the first and second echelons of our leadership, and it is their values which will set the American temper." These men and women are now retiring.

Whyte's description of the work ethic, so effective in business, is difficult to apply to retirement. When the old game is over, we must create a new game. Each of us must define the guidelines and rules by which we will play the new game. There are no corporate guidelines, no prescribed structure, no institutional objectives. Making the rules of this new game takes introspection.

Walter Cronkite, in an interview with *GQ* magazine, summed up the retirement problem:

"When I was out there and competing, and doing well in the competition, I was quite satisfied and happy. What is bothersome today is that I'm not competing at all. I'm not in the game. And that is annoying. I wouldn't say it's worrisome, because I know damn well I'm never going to be in the game. But that is annoying."

Cronkite is still in the game, but the game has changed. The game board also is changing for women. As more career women prepare to leave their corporate jobs, they are experiencing many of the same issues as men.

Take Sally, for example. As a senior partner in an accounting firm, sixty-three-year-old Sally Grimm had a fancy job title, an executive assistant, a hectic schedule, the companionship of colleagues, and the pride of being a pioneer in her profession. But when retirement loomed, she knew there would be gaps in her life. "What do you do all day?" she asked friends who had left the working world. "Then what do you do?" she pressed, unsatisfied by the first answer. "What do you do on weekends? How do you even know it's a weekend?"

Sally echoes laments of countless men and their fathers before them, who have struggled with retirement. Nevertheless, she is among the first of a generation of women to succeed in traditionally male professions. These women define themselves by their jobs, as much as by their families. They face retirement wondering: Without my work or the family I raised, who am I?

RESISTING THE TRANSITION TO THE WISDOM YEARS

The natural tendency when faced with pre-retirement fears is to resist the inevitable. Richard Ferry, CEO of the executive search firm Korn/Ferry, says, "Most of the guys I know never even use the "R" word. They move on to new things."

While this is an alternative, it often puts off the unavoidable and repeats the familiar. This makes sense, since most of us measure success by what we do. Without the traditional work-oriented sense of progress, how can we measure our worth?

For some, retirement is associated with death. Without a life-consuming job, many die after a short time. This group has a hard time believing and accepting that after so many decades of hard work, their careers are about to end. Being fired, let go, or forced to retire at a mandatory age, all feel the same—banished. In primitive societies, banishment is the equivalent of death. So is the pain of losing face or feeling insignificant.

For many, the reaction is anger—at themselves for not having planned what to do in the retirement years, at the organization for forcing them out, and at the younger generation for all their opportunities. As one top-level manager lamented, "It is painful. Even though you know it is a game, you learn the hard way. You had your turn and now a new guy gets his."

THE DROP FROM THE TOP

The loss of structure from the career-years applies to most retirees. The more senior the position, the more famous the athlete, the more successful the lawyer or politician, the tougher it is for a person to transition to retirement. For many, the thought of retiring is one of life's major traumas. It makes the top ten.

George Bush: Into the abyss of insignificance. In *New Passages: Mapping Your Life Across Time,* Gail Sheehy shows the impact of retirement on high-profile people in analysis of former President George Bush. Sheehy describes Bush's retirement apprehension: waking up election morning, November 1991, he was convinced he was going to win a second term. In fact, beyond a few vague statements about wanting to spend more time with his grandchildren, Bush had no backup plans about what to do with his life should he lose.

His stance persisted right up to the day he watched the movers cart their possessions out of the White House. Hyperactive and rarely reflective, his sense of identity was tied to the current title on his impressive resume. Being evicted from the White House and out of a job came as a devastating shock.

For the next several years, he followed the typical retirement pattern. He fished a lot, took his family on several cruises, and jetted with Barbara around the world from golf course to golf course. Sheehy maintains that some of his most loyal political advisors said privately that he was depressed and befuddled about what to do with his life, as if waiting to be given another mission. Unfortunately, it never happened until his son George W. tapped him and President Clinton to oversee the tsunami relief effort and the aftermath of Katrina's devastating effect on New Orleans.

Top executives are grieved to leave. Typically, at the pre-retirement stage, under guise of needing to cleanup some of their unfinished commitments, some people bargain to extend their retirement dates. Lee Iacocca began to feel the pre-retirement blues in the months leading up to his retirement. He initially stalled on selecting a successor and on setting a date for his departure. Then he was gone—to face an initial post retirement of frustration and emptiness. He says moving from Detroit to California and buying a house with his third wife in Bel Air was a disaster. His advice, "Pulling up roots was the hardest part. Hang onto something familiar, at least your house and your wife." He lost both in a nasty divorce. His conclusion is "Everybody says you've got to get ready financially. No, no, you've got to get ready psychologically."

Jack Welch, past CEO of General Electric, experienced a similar fate. Welch couldn't stand a lack of the familiar in retirement. In 1995, after nursing him through two heart attacks and a quintuple bypass, his wife Jane hoped there would be more time to enjoy together. As quoted in *People* magazine by one of Jane's colleagues, "It was like he [Jack] hit this solid wall of free time and he didn't like it. Suddenly he's going full-time again. She [Jane] felt cheated." Jack lost his wife in a divorce and then, in very public media coverage, the Board canceled many of his retirement perks. He tried to explain his post-retirement activities in the paperback reprint *Straight from the Gut.* A new wife, another book deal, a constant whirlwind of speeches, and a weekly column for *Business Week* keep him on a merry-go-round.

Sandy Weill is another larger-than-life figure who faced the mother of all executive transitions. He'd been going 180 miles an hour until he left the CEO's job, while remaining Citi's chairman. Suddenly he was down around zero. In a *Fortune* interview, he confessed, "The days drag. I'd have a meeting at nine in the morning and a phone call with someone at noon," he said, "And at 9:15 I'd be asking myself, 'what do I do until noon?'" As he talked, he gestured to his spacious, picture-packed quarters on the third floor of Citi's Manhattan headquarters and remarked, "There are only so many times I can pace around this office."

Jimmy Carter: Into the Wisdom Years. In contrast to George Bush's initial dispirited retirement, Sheehy points to the energetic post-presidency of Jimmy Carter. After Carter lost his re-election, he too was a shattered man. Despite being nominated for his efforts in the Camp David Accords, Carter was denied the Nobel Peace Prize and his political fortunes sank to an all-time low. He confessed to one reporter that he faced a potentially empty life. Returning home to Plains, Georgia, Sheehy says Carter, "found himself near financial ruin, a million dollars in debt, with the possibility of losing his farm and even his house."

Unlike Bush, however, Carter was determined to create a sense of meaning in his life. Within the first year of his retirement, both

Carter and his wife, Rosalyn, had profitable book contracts. Together they set up the Carter Center and became involved in championing various humanitarian projects. A talented mediator, Carter devoted his time and energy to several conflict resolution issues throughout the world, becoming an important resource for the presidencies of both George Bush and Bill Clinton. His post-retirement life is characterized by actively giving to others in creative ways. He was awarded the 2002 Nobel Peace Prize "for his decades of untiring effort to find peaceful solutions to international conflicts, to advance democracy and human rights, and to promote economic and social development."

HAPPINESS IN THE WISDOM YEARS

A seminal work on life transitions, Gail Sheehy's book *New Passages: Mapping Your Life Across Time* is a long-term study of Harvard Business School (HBS) Graduates from the class of 1949. At the group's fortieth reunion, she conducted one of her many follow-up surveys. Even though retired from conventional jobs, many were still working, some out of restlessness and others out of wanting to find more satisfying ways to use their time. The degree of happiness, as measured by her survey, produced some surprising results.

Productivity and personal relationships are key. None of the business-oriented factors (previous title, degree of success or failure, current net worth, amount of work in post-retirement) significantly affected happiness. The one variable that produced most unhappy HBS retirees was having "not gone on to do anything productive beyond pleasing themselves." Conversely, the HBS respondents who enjoyed the highest well-being reached out for new adventures and had developed heartfelt personal relationships. They viewed retirement as an opportunity to add depth and richness to their lives.

The choice: Into the abyss or onto the Wisdom Years? The eventual question any retiree faces is: "Who are you when you are no longer defined by your work?" While my dad's experience may be an extreme case, there are many variations on his theme. Each retiree's experience is different, but the unavoidable problems are similar.

Dr. Shoshana Zuboff, a Harvard social scientist an expert on wealth, work, and identity, warns about all work and no play. She concludes that for many people there is no "self" outside their work identities. She notes that people are more spacious and complex creatures than the superficial identities tied to their jobs. There is a difference between who we are and what we do. Further, she makes the distinction between personal connections based on human dignity and those in the commercial world based on a person's usefulness.

The litmus test for a retirement life worth living may be a middle ground between the abyss of insignificance and a whirlwind life jam-packed with trips and social engagements. Often semi-retired workaholics are driven to work, because it is all they know. They are not having fun, but they think they are. Real fun is not driven by a frenetic energy to prove anything. With real fun, time melts away and joy is the by-product. There is an inner peace, often not understood because the feeling is new, personal, and hard to explain. Achieving a state of inner peace takes time.

The story of Jack Welch's transition, or Iacocca's troubled retirement years, or Sandy Weill's pre-retirement anxiety, or my dad's inability to transition, offers a cautionary note to anyone who is plunged into retirement unprepared. But Jimmy Carter's triumphant retirement is an inspiration to us all.

PONDER THIS

Before leaving this chapter, ask yourself these questions:

- Who do I admire in his/her retirement?
- What aspects of that person's retirement are noteworthy?
- How can I incorporate those admirable aspects into my retirement?

CHAPTER FOUR: BELIEFS SHAPE REALITY

Returning home from a Mediterranean vacation aboard a replica clipper ship, George had some time for quiet introspection. He reflected on a pattern of behavior that became obvious while taking taxis during the vacation. When a taxi driver loaded and unloaded the bags, George insisted on helping. It's the same when he is sick or lost and needs directions. He resists letting people help him. Thinking about this tendency, George concluded he feels uncomfortable being dependent on others. Why does this happen? George reasoned that his core beliefs about his overall competency shape his behaviors.

We label the strongly held truths and fears we carry into the Wisdom Years "legacy beliefs." Each of us has a set of legacy beliefs acquired from our family of origin and early life experiences. Legacy beliefs are strong ideas about our existence that result in engrained patterns of behavior. While many such behaviors bring success, many are inappropriate in the post-career years. We do what is comfortable and familiar, but that is the cruel trap. Retirement is not business as usual. What worked in the past is of little use in the Wisdom Years.

Beliefs, thoughts, expectations, ideas, and intentions create both physical objects and psychological events. For example, it is easy to identify personal belief structures when discussing religion or politics. With these beliefs, we create elaborate social structures of communities, nations, and individual relationships. Further, they influence our choices of political positions, friends, party affiliations, and where we put our energy.

THOUGHTS AS CREATIVE ENERGY

In the Wisdom Years, career and kids are behind us. Acceptance of retirement is influenced by self-image, views about old age, and the ability to understand and modify. There are new measures of success, such as fulfillment, meaning, and joy from new activities. These affect the sense of well-being and happiness.

Thoughts have creative potential. Beautiful thoughts build beautiful events and material things. The intention manifests in physical reality. If we focus on ugly things, we attract more ugliness into our lives. On the other hand, if we view unpleasant circumstances in a positive light, we can change reality. By choosing how we experience even the worst of circumstances, we structure the world to rise above unpleasant situations—we are inner focused.

Whatever the programming, the mind does its job. Thus we must resist the urge to use past negative strategies or dwell on hurts, mistakes, errors, and fears. Thoughts produce the expected reality. When we change the way we look at things, the things we look at change.

THE PROCESS OF THE MIND

It is vital to understand the sequence of the mind. It uses a recognizable, yet complex four-step process to create individual reality. The four components are thoughts, imagination (visualization), emotion, and action.

Thoughts. We use words to describe what is stored in the mind's database. Each is a slight variation of the core word belief. Ideas, visual images, memories, intention, truth, conviction, certainty, and fears are thoughts. These are the raw materials of the mental process. When they surface in consciousness, they trigger imagination.

Imagination. We form images in the mind, especially of things not seen or experienced directly. In the mind's eye, we visualize thoughts and turn them into pictures. These include fears and desires, such as boats, cars, and vacations. One way to create a desire is to place a picture for easy viewing, for example, visualizing owning a boat. Act as though you already have it. Salespeople use this technique in preparation for making a sale—they see the customer placing the order or signing the contract. Athletes see themselves singing *The Star Spangled Banner* when receiving their gold medal.

Emotions and action. Visualization stimulates the imagination and produces emotional energy, subtly triggering actions and a whole host of unpredictable events. In business, the goal-setting process has its underpinning in this same process. A corporate vision statement is an idea for creating a desired future. "I have a dream," is no different.

Through continued focus, attention, imagination, and emotion, action is set in motion. Ideas can become experienced reality.

The physical world is neutral. It has one of everything. The mind is unable to distinguish between good and bad thoughts and selects whatever it is directed to seek. The good, the bad, and the ugly are all produced by the same process.

FEAR—FALSE EVIDENCE APPEARING REAL

We will use fear to show the mind's process in action, since fear is the most potent form of belief. If you have a fear and dwell on it, your imagination conjures up different threatening scenarios and you attract the very thing you fear. The emotion of fear is a product of belief. From one significant emotional event, you extrapolate the experience to cover all future events. The stronger the fear, the higher the probability it will happen. Thus, fear runs a part of your life.

Fear is false evidence appearing real, unless truly justified. If you fear heights and are climbing a ladder or walking on a high footbridge, you freeze up. The fear actually puts you in more danger because of your imagination. The ladder and footbridge are safe, but your emotional reaction creates the danger. The core component behind all fears is the question: Will I be able to handle the situation? If you have doubts, watch out.

Root causes of fear. Psychological fears fall into two major categories: losing control and not gaining approval. Wanting control or wanting approval is the driver behind the fear. You may have some of both, but one dominates. Do you flee physically? (fear of losing control) Do you maintain your ground and fight? Or try to keep the peace? (fear of not gaining approval) What about your partner? Usually, your partner has the opposite characteristic.

Control and approval are modern day versions of core survival mechanisms. These are hard-wired in the brain. Even though we are not in physical danger, this DNA is a powerful trigger. Instead, we substitute emotional threats for physical ones and react as if they are life threatening. These can be threats to our system of beliefs about religion, politics, or anything that assaults the ego. Ego death is the root cause of every psychological fear.

Fears result from life experiences that become patterns. People who continually fail, have the fear of failing again. When they fail again, they justify the fear. Likewise, those who consider themselves victims or believe people are not trustworthy, attract those who are untrustworthy and will victimize them. The unconscious belief creates what is feared.

Fears in the Wisdom Years. Retirees typically have three fears: loss of importance, finances, and health. Chapter Eight covers the loss of importance in detail and discusses how we can transition from outer-driven importance to personal significance and happiness.

Money worries in retirement loom so large, they fuel a huge financial planning industry. For many, the fear of running out of money is a real possibility. However, even with a tidy nest egg, this fear can lurk in the background. If not recognized, self-sabotaging behavior can result in reckless spending or a reclusive miser who dies leaving millions in the bank.

The health issue is attached to the fear of growing old and being dependent on others. The thought of old age brings on the image of death. The realities of growing older are often masked by denial: this will not happen to me. The loss of youth means we are not as robust as before and may not have the stamina to do things as in the past. Balance may be off, so we may resist the very movement and activities that can help stave off the vicissitudes associated with getting older. Staying active physically and mentally is the key—and learning to accept help from others when needed.

The underlying element of fear is the assumption that happiness depends on not losing anything. Thus, the loss of any asset means diminished pleasure and satisfaction. Other retirement losses include: loss of privilege, position, title, reputation, relationships, possessions, influence, power, love, sexual attractiveness, status, opportunity, and mental acuity.

The power of the paradox. It is important to remember: the mind's job is to produce whatever is asked of it. Thus the paradox of fear: we get what we fear. Fortunately, the opposite also is true. For example, if you believe people are trustworthy, you will experience trustworthiness. The mind does not care how the belief is labeled—

good ones and bad ones get the same attention. That means we have the power to turn it around—acknowledge and accept fear—then replace it with positive beliefs.

LEGACY BELIEFS ARE NOT FACTS

Legacy beliefs are the filters through which we selectively view the physical world. This basket of unconscious thought controls our attitudes about religion, personal worth, how to treat people, politics, and what is fearful.

The behavior patterns structured around legacy beliefs are invisible. These beliefs spring alive with experience, thus we think of them as a facts, rather than beliefs. Any idea we accept as truth, fits a legacy belief.

Below are examples of legacy beliefs some people may hold true:

- You are at the mercy of your past, because your personality was formed when a child.
- You and your group have the truth and no one else has it.
- You will grow sicker and frailer as you age.
- Pleasurable experiences produce happiness.
- You cannot train an old dog to do new tricks.
- Good things come only if you work hard.
- You can't trust people.

The outer world is a reflection of our inner world. Our sense of joy, sorrow, health, or illness—all of these are created by our beliefs. If we believe that a given situation should make us unhappy, it will and the unhappiness reinforces the condition.

Maintaining legacy beliefs feels safe because they are familiar. But in reality, unexamined beliefs are dangerous since they may be severely limiting. They narrowly shape what and how we experience life. Sticking stubbornly to legacy beliefs is not a virtue if they limit us from growing. It's like driving a car with the brakes on. Understanding our legacy beliefs takes introspection and effort.

CHANGING PERSONAL REALITY

It is critical to understand the power of beliefs in shaping personal experienced reality. Be willing to say, "I learn about myself from the reality I create." In other words, "The world around me is a reflection of my beliefs. It is a mirror image. My judgments of what I experience are about me."

The world has a complete range of good/evil, black/white, rich/poor. Experience has nothing to do with the physical reality. Physical reality just provides the backdrop and the stimuli. Through context and bias, you provide the physical reality and meaning. So, judgment is about yourself, not the other person or the event.

Jane Roberts best expresses these concepts in her book, *The Nature of Personal Reality.* She makes two points. Life is about what you create and how you learn from these experiences.

"You are, however, in physical existence using your body as a medium for learning expression. You are unique. Many of you for your own reasons pursue courses that do not involve an even development of abilities, and overall balanced picture, for example, but choose to express and experiment with certain qualities [beliefs] to the exclusion of others. If all of your beliefs, not just your 'fortunate' ones, were not materialized, you would never thoroughly understand on a physical level that your ideas create your reality [experience]. If only your 'positive' beliefs were materialized then you would never clearly comprehend the power of your thought, for you would not completely experience its physical results."

Using our bodies as mediums of learning, we engage in lifelong learning. Since each thought has a result, we must take responsibility for the good and the not-so-good. If we simply say, "That's life," we are not being accountable and leave ourselves at the mercy of events over which it appears we have no control. Change the way you look at things and the things you look at change.

TRY THIS

Change your beliefs. The past existed in many ways, yet you experienced only one version of it—your version. By changing the past in your mind, you can change its nature and its effect. Here's how.

Take a particularly disturbing event in your past. Imagine it is not only wiped out, but replaced by another event of a more beneficial nature. This replacement process must be done with great vividness and emotional content and repeated many times. It's what world-class athletes do to improve their techniques. It is not a self-deception. Your chosen event becomes a *probable event* which did happen, though it is not the event you chose to experience in your past.

Realize, events not physically perceived or experienced are valid. They are real within your own psychological environment. There are unlimited probable future events for which you are now setting the groundwork. The nature of the thoughts and feelings you originate and those you habitually experience set a pattern.

If you are aware of your experienced reality, you will understand it is a reflection of your beliefs. Change the beliefs and change what happens to you in the future. By being aware of your actions, you can alter your behaviors and grow in new directions.

Many of the legacy beliefs we bring to the retirement years need a critical review of their appropriateness and effectiveness. The skill required is openness and introspection.

Visualize the ideal. What might your ideal retirement be like? What pictures form in your mind as yourself living the retirement life of your dreams? Write down the elements of your vision and their associated emotions. Read the final analysis to a partner or trusted friend. Listen to his/her feedback. Be open to the responses and questions to help clarify this picture of the ideal. With it, you are on your way to disassociating from your legacy beliefs, replacing them with a set ensuring happiness in retirement.

PONDER THIS

Take a moment and reflect on the questions below. Consider recording your thoughts, insights, and ah-ha's or discuss these with a significant other in your life.

- What were my initial retirement beliefs?
- What were my partner's retirement beliefs?
- What are my beliefs now?
- How have my belief changed?
- How have my partner's beliefs changed?
- What is working? What is not? Why?
- Can I trace "disappointment emotions" to the core beliefs I hold?
- Is there a logical transition strategy?

CHAPTER FIVE: FROM OTHER-DIRECTED TO SELF-DIRECTED STRUCTURE

Retired at age sixty after a long career as a nuclear physicist, Dean initially roamed from room to room, so restless, he couldn't even read. Sometimes he'd putter doing small household repair projects and run errands. He tried one volunteer job, but it failed to satisfy his needs. Although concerned, his wife realized she couldn't provide a structure for him. Then he found volunteer work as a mediator for the court system, added a weekly golf game, and began consulting in a field he loves. Although some of these activities were his wife's original suggestions, Dean has adopted them as his own.

Dean made the transition from the other-directed structure of the career world to the self-directed open timescape of the retirement world, albeit with some bumps along the way. Becoming *self-directed* is a process of unlearning and relearning. Since much of our lives reflects what others have wanted us to do, we are used to external influences and being *other-directed.*

The learning years. We didn't choose the beliefs that structure our lives—they were given to us to make order out of the confusion. We accepted the information passed down by our parents, siblings, teachers, and grandparents, adapting to their rules. If not, we paid the consequences, perhaps punishment—either physical or psychological.

Since we wanted approval and the feeling of being nurtured, we learned what it took. This need for approval—the motivation to learn—conditioned us to be good children and good workers.

The performing years. During our performing years, we acquired another set of beliefs, fashioned by our social, religious, political, and business institutions. Thirty or forty career years adhering to prescribed policies provided powerful conditioning. The values, mores, beliefs, suppressions, and fears gained validity over time and became living truths.

FACING THE VOID

There is a curious fact: the busier you were, the more structured your day, the more time you had, and the more you did. Not so in the post-career years. Now large blocks of unstructured free time are available and nothing much gets done. There are many feelings associated with this new reality. It is wonderful not to rush in the morning and to have time to luxuriate in reading the paper and a second cup of coffee.

But this wasn't the feeling I had. I felt uneasy with unstructured free time. When I left corporate life for my own consulting practice, I felt guilty at 8 AM if I wasn't at my desk working. Even now, it feels like cheating when I take a short afternoon nap.

Free time feels like a threat. We want structure. So activity of any kind is an attempt to fill the void. We may start projects with enthusiasm only to put them up on the shelf. The half-finished scrapbook or photo album is a good example.

The pressure of career deadlines often motivated us to produce our best work. Without deadlines, it can be hard to get going. "If I don't do it today I'll do it tomorrow. I don't have to worry. Pretty soon it will get done." Time slips away; projects are put off and ennui creeps in. To lessen the boredom and to feel something more, we may start drinking earlier in the afternoon (sundowners disease). Unless filled with purposeful self-directed effort, time can become an enemy as the shadow structure takes over and negatively dominates behavior.

EMERGING SHADOW STRUCTURE

When you experience the loss of formal career structures—a place to go, a dress code, time schedules, following through on commitments, and the do's and don'ts of business—a default structure kicks in—your *shadow structure* learned during the performing years. It runs silently in the background, influencing your life and choices. Unless aware of it, you don't know it exists—*you don't know you don't know.* You cannot see it. It is not as obvious as other-directed rules and social norms. It is an internal structure of thoughts, emotions, beliefs, and expectations. It comes into full bloom when your work identity fades and another identity clamors for a life of its own. Some call it the ego, but, it is more than that.

Your shadow structure is more powerful than society's rules because it is steeped in the subconscious database. Made up of legacy beliefs, your shadow structure is your *operating system*, running in the background like a computer program.

Consider the age-old debate about how much of human behavior comes from nature versus nurture. Assume that half of your operating system is hard-wired with genetic DNA and the other half is programmed by a lifetime of experiences. Your acquired database runs in the background, full of personal characterizations, dramatizations, and displays of your beliefs. To start your personal growth, you must *know yourself* and understand the contents of your database.

OBSTACLES TO BEING SELF-DIRECTED

Examining our acquired beliefs will illuminate how we react to life's events and will help us appreciate how shadow beliefs are obstacles to well-being. We accept a suggestion given by another only if it fits with our own ideas. The opposite also is true—we reject ideas that conflict with our beliefs. Because we are not conscious of our beliefs, the impact of everyday life events seems normal and natural. When we examine and understand the psychological structure behind our behaviors, we see how they shape our social and personal realities.

Repeating the familiar. Consider my experience at my fifty-fifth high school reunion. Harris was a small man, well-dressed, tan, and working the room. I didn't know him in high school and was unaware that he played football. Within a few minutes into the conversation I felt his neediness to be recognized as somebody and important. He professed he was captain of the football team, better than most, had gone through three wives, and was still playing the field. There wasn't a real person behind the façade, just a pathetic little man reliving the past to feel important.

Familiar patterns of behavior result from strongly held beliefs. Consider a man who gets divorced and then marries a carbon copy of his previous spouse. He may do this four or five times, hoping this time it will be different. He is unable to see how he sets himself up for more trauma and drama. He attracts the familiar because it looks right. This is programming others can see, but to which he is blind.

Why can't he see the problems he creates for himself? To him, it looks perfectly normal. If he thought his behavior was wrong, he would not do it! Yet, this is not the case. A string of divorces defines his life and he doesn't have a clue as to why.

Consider the scenario of the retiree having problems with adult children or money, and is lost as to why. It may be easy for others to see, but it is hard for individuals to modify their automatic behaviors. They continue their patterns because they look right, they are familiar, and this gives them comfort.

There also is a high or inner pleasure reinforcing many behaviors. For example, people get pleasure from harboring resentments, being the martyr, playing the victim, or from controlling others. Controllers get a distorted sense of pleasure when manipulating others. For victims needing approval, the motivation is *now will you love me?* These drivers reinforce unhealthy behaviors and explain why it is so difficult to give them up.

The activity trap. One obvious strategy for filling the void is to keep busy. For successful people, gratifying work represents an integral component of life. We must find something other than activities to provide that same business high.

There are two kinds of activities: those with a purpose and those for pleasure. Enjoyable, leisure activities rarely fill the void. Dining out, trips to faraway destinations, long walks, and movies are pleasurable activities. But when pleasure is the only goal, each new adventure has to top the last and in the long-term it all loses its luster.

A gratifying life is steeped in purpose and structure, with pleasure as a by-product. Combining pleasure and purpose is desirable. For example, business trips had purpose and structure with the added bonus of golfing and social interaction.

Feeling important. In the Wisdom Years, we shed dependence on other-directed approval and find joy and fulfillment from being self-directed. It is not an easy to transition from *being somebody* and important to *being just anybody*. Feeling important requires an understanding of where you have been and where you are now. Your successes, your standing in the community, your friendships, your earning power, your busy schedule, your feeling of being somebody—will look more important, more valuable, and indeed more indispensable as you attempt to find your way without a career identity.

The one with the most toys wins. Another way to feel excitement and establish a self-image of importance is to collect stuff. A few years into retirement, however, buried by stuff, many report they spend too much time just managing the logistics of their lives.

Consider John's story, for example. Having not figured out what would challenge his abilities and energize him again, John had a hard time beating back conflicting emotions. He had freedom of choice about how to spend his time, yet lacked motivation to do anything in particular. With this combination, it was easy to slide into a passive role. He ran around to stay busy, buying the latest gadgets he didn't need and opting for the TV's sports channel when bored. After a while, his life was built solely around pleasure and acquiring stuff and he experienced ennui and unhappiness.

Reiterating Gail Sheehy's Harvard Business School (HBS) study: "The most unhappy HBS retirees had not gone on to do anything productive beyond pleasing themselves." Consider Pinocchio's experience with Pleasure Island. The Disney classic depicts what can happen in a life filled merely with pleasure. Only when his conscience wakes him up does Pinocchio find his real self. Thus he is transformed from a wooden puppet of life's circumstances to a being blessed with a human spirit.

Picking up roots. Retirement brings the opportunity to move to a dream location or a warmer climate. Moving seems like a good idea. Why stay in the same old place?

Take Harry's story, for example. For years, a retirement dream house was an exciting project as Harold worked with architects, builders, and decorators. Then his wife Sally encountered a problem with their decision to move to a desert community. While it was only an hour-and-a-half away, the distance changed their lives. Their circle of friends, familiar neighbors, church affiliation, and the routine of just shopping for groceries changed. While folks visited them initially, Sally found she was making trips back to the former neighborhood to connect with the friends and activities. All the while she was thinking, "We should never have moved."

As retirees realize that relocation means starting over again, the flight to Florida, Arizona, and California is starting to abate. Replacing familiar community life and relationships just when the spouse is losing long-time business associates is a double loss affecting both partners.

CHANGING HABITS

Patterns are conditioned from years of business experience and childhood experiences. No wonder the retired manager begins organizing the kitchen, questioning the household budgeting process, and treating the spouse as an administrative assistant. Habits can limit new experiences and lead to continued sadness, frustration, or disappointment.

Some habit patterns are so subtle, we hardly know they are operating. Being on autopilot allows us to function without having to think about what we are doing. Probably ninety percent of what we do is done without conscious thought. We perform hundreds of habitual tasks each day.

In the performance years, our habits, routines, and schedules were so well constructed, we could awaken, dress, eat breakfast, catch a plane, rent a car, and arrive at a client's office without ever having to think. Now we have to learn ways of doing things differently from what has worked in the past – recognizing we may still be on automatic pilot and not know it.

The loss of youthfulness, however, is a great teacher. As we age, we lose many natural abilities. Our eyesight weakens, our hearing is reduced, our stamina wanes, our balance is compromised, reaction times slow, and a "senior moment" clouds where we put our car keys. All of these God-given gifts change in the aging process and force us to become more aware of what we are doing.

Become an objective observer. The position as an objective observer allows us to become aware of the connection between our thoughts and the expectations that birthed them. Observe what is happening and ask: What is it in me, that causes me to experience things in this manner? Asking this question brings us one step closer to being aware of our patterns and structuring a different lifestyle.

STRUCTURING A DIFFERENT LIFESTYLE

When we become self-directed, we structure our lives differently. We override and replace legacy beliefs—ideas and behavior patterns that do not serve personal growth—with a new set of insights driven by inner truths. The job is to discover and act on what's *in here*, rather than believe we are controlled by what's *out there*.

Self-directedness is essentially an entrepreneurial quality—something most large organizations breed out of people. To create personal structure requires refocused action. Measures of success are many—replacing business associates with a new circle of acquaintances, ensuring personal connections with family and friends, and creating a balance of pleasurable, fulfilling, gratifying, and meaningful activities.

During the Wisdom Years, we add new insights to an established foundation, thus increasing the range of opportunities for self-expression. The ideal is to be in the world—not necessarily influenced by it. This requires experimentation and introspection, essential qualities for replacing the *juice of business* with the *highs of living*.

This transition is marked by a growing concern with spiritual matters and a sense of being in touch with the inner forces guiding most decisions. At this stage of life, many of us become socially conscious and extend our inner-direction beyond ourselves. A profound sense of societal responsibility leads us to support causes such as conservation, environmentalism, and a global understanding of how best to live together. We may be attracted to simple living and the natural or take up lives of voluntary simplicity. Or we may do volunteer work. We assume a high degree of self-reliance, successfully replacing the norms, expectations, and imposed structure of the career years.

Retirement is the invitation to take a journey of self-discovery. The "can'ts" and "won'ts" are unfounded fears. As the Nike ad says, "Just do it." It's your new job.

TRY THIS

Visualize your self at the end of your ideal day—identify how you would like to structure your time—percentage of your time spent in personal maintenance, socializing, hobbies, sports, recreation, relaxing, resting, recharging, service to others, or a business enterprise. Focus on the ideal. Watch how the unconscious takes over and says, "You can't do that.....you don't have the skill....that would be boring....you don't know anybody.... you won't feel important doing that".....on and on and on.

PONDER THIS

Before leaving this chapter, ask yourself these questions:

- How do I fill large blocks of unstructured free time now?
- Am I caught up in a constant activity trap to fill the void?
- Do I recognize how shadow structures pull at me to recreate and relive the past, who I was and my importance?

CHAPTER SIX: FROM SOCIAL IDENTITY TO PERSONAL IDENTITY

"At different times in my life, I have introduced myself as a submariner, a farmer, a warehouseman, a state senator, a governor, or even a president, if that was necessary. I might have added where I lived, but that was about it. Now, even though not holding a steady job, I could reply...that I am a professor, an author, a fly-fisherman, or a woodworker. I could add an American, a southerner, a Christian, a husband, or a grandfather." Jimmy Carter

From the statement above, it is clear former president Jimmy Carter is aware of the many roles he has taken in his life—and now he can add "a Nobel Peace-prize winner" to his list. In the career years, our roles are easily defined and become inextricably tied to our identities. What happens when we retire? How do we answer that ubiquitous question, *What do you do?*

Judith Viorst sums it up with these words, "Work shores up our identity; it anchors both the private and social self; it defines that self to itself and to the world. And lacking a workplace to go to, a circle of colleagues to connect with, a task to confirm our competence, a salary that puts a value on that competence, a job description that serves as a shorthand way of telling a stranger who we are, we may—when we have retired—start to ask, with growing anxiety, 'Who am I?'" This excellent summary of the retirement experience is from Viorst's book, *Necessary Losses.*

To speak of identity—one's *self*—is a complicated matter. At any given moment, we have several different versions of ourselves. We wear different faces for different occasions. Some might argue, we have as many selves as people we meet. To make sense of our different personas, it is helpful to categorize them as belonging to either social identity or personal identity.

SOCIAL IDENTITY VERSUS PERSONAL IDENTITY

During the performing years, social identity is tied to what we do, titles, salaries, a bonus package, and the perks. As a management consultant, when I first meet people, I slot them into work categories. It is a nasty habit formed over the years to quickly calibrate an organization, its problems, and the maturity of its people. I find myself doing this with people, even though it is inappropriate.

We do the same thing at social gatherings, like a wedding or a dinner party. Categorization allows for good initial conversation and we feel comfortable discovering similarities. This is the classic method of determining a person's social identity.

The economic scoreboard. One way business people calculate social identity is a relative peer ranking—how much money they make. Being on top in Fortune's list of high-earning executives is a status symbol. It is not about the money; it's a person's position on the scoreboard. Even with satisfactory pensions and stock options, we are reminded of the importance of social identity when these perks are taken away. The same is true of material wealth. Huge houses and lots of stuff are tied to identity—the want to have versus the need to have.

Emergence of personal identity. The ability to be aware and ask the fundamental question Who am I? distinguishes us from animals, which are conscious but not self-conscious. In retirement, we remain who we always were, but social identity is obscured.

Much of the frustration in early retirement comes from lacking a clear purpose and knowing who we are—really knowing. In some cases, we feel frustrated and we question, Now what do I do? These questions are rooted in the desire to understand the authentic self—discover who we are.

As social identity diminishes, the significance of personal identity and discovery of the authentic self emerges. Discovery occurs through introspection—exploring the deeper layers of identity. It's like peeling layers of an onion. As part of the lifelong journey, self-discovery is a continual process.

Walt Whitman wrote some encouraging words, "Re-examine all you have been told in school or church or in any book, dismiss what ever insults your own soul, and your very flesh shall be a great poem."

Becoming a great poem takes work in three particular areas.

RECOGNIZING AUTOPILOT BEHAVIORS

Chapter four on legacy beliefs discussed how pervasive beliefs shape personal truths. Beliefs about who we are begin in childhood, when, to be accepted and loved, we adopt the best and worst of our parents. These soft-wired behavior patterns combine with our hard-wired DNA to shape identity.

Couple this conditioning with the role we assumed in a competitive career world and it becomes evident our social identity is not who we are. We are much more. There is deeper I-ness, a spiritual core.

Reinforced by experience, beliefs form the habitual patterns known as automatic-pilot behaviors, the behaviors repeated over and over. These behaviors occur spontaneously, not out of choice.

For example, we may respond to life's situations by becoming anxious or remaining calm, we may be generous or withholding, strict or lenient, controlling or permissive, optimistic or pessimistic, available or unavailable, talkative or quiet, encouraging or discouraging, intuitive or reasoning, rational or irrational, and impulsive or cautious. These are only a few examples of autopilot behaviors, all of which have great impact.

The self has awareness and, through objective observation, can rediscover its authentic self. The ability to be aware is inherent in human nature and, along with an analytical mind, can be used to diminish the effects of autopilot tendencies.

IDENTIFYING ROLES

To answer the Who am I? question, we must identify the various roles we play. Adult roles formed throughout the working years have the greatest pull on awareness. Since performance behaviors are constantly reinforced, we build our images around them. We may identify with the job aspects of personality, such as being aggressive or competitive and thus function accordingly. Athletes identify with their bodies. They talk in terms of sensations; in other words, they function as if they are their bodies. Women identify more with their emotions and express how they feel.

Consider for a moment these facts: you have a body but you are more than your body. You have a mind, but you are more than your mind. You had a career, but clearly this is not who you were. Taking this process further, you can see that it is possible to disengage, or "dis-identify," from other traits and aspects of yourself such as desires, roles, impulses, habits, beliefs, fears, material possessions or just about anything. If you are able to do this, you are left then with only "I-consciousness." You become the observer, disengaging from fears, annoying thoughts, and inappropriate roles, thus short circuiting autopilot wiring. Through intention, we gain freedom and the choice to keep or let go of any personality trait that does not serve us.

The over-identification with either a role or dominant personality characteristic leads to a sense of loss, even depression, when it is gone. This is true of the professional who retires from a private practice, the cop who no longer wears the badge, the athlete who grows old and loses physical strength, or the mother whose children have grown and left her nest. Some actors become so identified with specific characters, they forget who they are and only experience themselves in the roles they play. Executives, mothers, and others anticipate these life-changing transitions as partial death. It is. It is the death of a social identity.

MANAGING PERSONALITY CHARACTERISTICS

If we are unaware of our personality traits and do not manage them well, they end up managing us. One technique is to give each personality characteristic a name, then claim it, and tame it if gets out of line.

Naming. Unlike an actor, the average person doesn't consciously change roles easily. We may wear roles for a long time, such as student, executive, father, father-in-law, and the list goes on. Disassociating from the roles and identifying with the core essence are important steps in overcoming the loss of social identity. In addition, identifying various aspects eliminates confusion. If we label each aspect and identify the dimensions and characteristics, we can bring each quality to light.

Claiming. Next, we must be willing to claim the characteristics as our own, both the good qualities and those that might be distasteful — the autocrat, the sarcastic, the toy boy, the egocentric, the braggart, the performer, just to name a few. The cast of characters makes up the strengths and weaknesses for which we are known.

We are whole human beings, including all the things we like and dislike about ourselves. We possess both the good and the bad. In order to have "goodness" we need to acknowledge existence of the dark side—the fears, addictions, and compulsive behaviors we try to hide.

Claiming overcomes denial. Whatever you resist persists. There are aspects of yourself you must own. By claiming them, you bring them into the light of awareness. It becomes clear that judgments may be reflections of personal beliefs—especially about the dark side.

Taming. Having named them and claimed them, we take the last step and tame them. Taming doesn't mean controlling them; rather it means to direct them, to consciously allow them to play their parts when appropriate. Each personality aspect needs a voice. If denied expression, it becomes frustrated and works against the better good. Just like children, if ignored they will act out with sabotaging behavior.

Consider that each has a voice and wants to be heard. Suppose you are dealing with a "controller" sub-personality. The controller needs to control everything and everybody. He is uncomfortable when he is not in control.

To tame an aspect of your personality, enter into a dialogue with it. Take the "controller" sub-personality. You might start the dialogue by finding out why he does what he does. At first he may say, "I want you to do what I ask all the time." And you may say, "Why do you want that?" By continuing to ask "why," by trying to understand the reasons behind the request, you are able to move to the root of this behavior. There is always resistance when probing the ego, but you may get this aspect to admit, "When I'm in control I feel order in my life."

Since all behavior is grounded in beliefs, you might find the controlling behavior is the result of an unhappy childhood growing up under the influence of alcoholic parents. Not trusting their behavior, not feeling safe, not knowing when they would "lose it," is often what produces controlling behavior. Wanting to control things before they get out of control makes perfect sense. If you recognize that under the need for control there is often a need to feel safe, you can find ways to satisfy this need. You can say, "I can't let you run everybody, I can't let you dominate others, but I understand your need to feel safe and I can help you with that." You are saying, "I can't give you what you want, but I'll give you what you really need." He might respond with, "I never really wanted obsessive control anyway; I just wanted to feel safe."

In time, with experience and understanding, this aspect of you will realize it can handle chaos and learns to trust itself. It grows up, in time becomes its own parent, and controls its own behavior. You begin to trust this aspect of yourself, knowing you are responsible for making yourself feel safe.

To respond appropriately to an aspect of yourself, you must understand the aspect in depth. This is where dialoguing helps. Once you see that the controller isn't really a controller, but is just someone who is afraid, you can help him feel safe.

No one consciously chooses to act inappropriately. We become blind to behaviors we acquire along life's path that feel right. Dialoguing is a process for becoming aware of those behaviors.

When we move to this level of awareness, we become increasingly able to choose which personality aspects we want to express or eliminate. Until then, we are on autopilot, controlled by aspects of our personality, the beliefs behind them, and their particular good or undesirable qualities.

Every quality within is available as we play out life's dramas. Being in charge is enabling and provides the greatest freedom of expression to reach full potential. This level is described as being self-actualized or being a well-integrated person. The process of naming, claiming, and taming facilitates answering the question, Who am I? and uncovers the center of identity, the I-ness.

TRY THIS

Who are you? Find a place where you can work quietly and undisturbed. On a clean sheet of paper write, "Who am I" at the top and note the date. Then, repeatedly ask yourself, "Who am I?" Write down whatever comes to mind. Don't think about the answers, write whatever comes up. Write as quickly as possible as the thoughts pop into your awareness.

As you again ask yourself the question, "Who am I?" think about the many roles you play in life's ongoing play. Your list will be long and touch all aspects of your life. Ten to fifteen minutes is a reasonable amount of time to identify the many facets of your personality.

You should now have a list of your many personality elements, aspects of yourself, roles, and other personal and social descriptions with which you identify yourself. This awareness is a first step in uncovering your authentic self and gaining personal freedom from the roles, you choose to play or not to play in life.

My personal list leads me to identify aspects of myself I label as Pushy Pete and Competitive Charlie. I decided to first talk with Pushy Pete. The feedback: He thought I was a bit too competitive, too driven, and too obsessive about life. Wow! Immediately I went into DENIAL, which is translated as (Don't Even Notice I Am Lying), rationalizing myself out of one corner only to be put into another by his logic and persistence. I relented and realized my beliefs about being competitive. Competitive people, I believed, were rude, pushy, greedy, and under certain circumstances unethical. Because of dialoguing with Pushy Pete, I sensed these characteristics in my makeup and it's okay. I know that sometimes these behaviors are appropriate and I am in control and can choose when to bring them to my aid.

Next, I chatted with Competitive Charlie and inquired about the quality he represented. He said, "Another side of your competitiveness." As we talked, it became clear he was energetic, full of enthusiasm, and a hard worker. His gifts were persistence and wanting to prove he was competent by winning. I asked him how he had helped me in the past; his reply, "In the past, I have served you well. Your success in overcoming dyslexia and struggling in school can be attributed to my persistence and willingness to strive." We talked about his negative qualities i.e. treating all activities as competitive challenges and focusing too much on the goal while not spending enough time smelling the roses. He counseled me to enjoy my retirement years, to slow down, and enjoy the process. I realized that competing all the time, especially with other men didn't serve me anymore. My job was to form bonds based on a friendship, not on how fast I could swim or bike.

Dialogue with your authentic self. Start the dialogue with the first strong personality who stands out on your list. Ask his/her name or assign a name. Remember, you've selected an aspect of yourself. You may have energy about this aspect; it may be one you would rather not own. You may have had feedback in the past about it. If denial kicks in, stop and think about your autopilot response. If you feel like rationalizing your way out, claim it anyway, and answer the eight questions below.

- What is the name of this personality aspect?

- What does the person representing it look like? What emotions is s/he feeling? What are you feeling?
- What aspect of you does s/he represent?
- What is s/he trying to teach? What are his/her gifts?
- How has this personality aspect helped in the past?
- How can you claim it as part of you?
- What action must you take to tame this sub-personality when it gets out of hand?
- What are the consequences if you let this aspect dominate your life?

PONDER THIS

The I of I. Every quality in us—every aspect—is available as we play out life's dramas. Taking responsibility allows the freedom of expression required to reach full potential. It is described as being self-actualized or being a well-integrated person. The process of naming, claiming, and taming all aspects of your personality uncovers the center of identity, the I-ness.

Think for a moment about your personal identity. If you were to strip away all the trappings of a social identity, how would you describe the authentic you, your I-ness? Give it a try. Answer these questions.

What does it mean that you are "The I of the I?" Here is a hint. Start with the premise that I am more than an animal and more than a human being. If so, what am I?

- How do I express my personal identity?
- How can I describe my personal identity without social labels?
- How would others know if I am expressing my personal identity?

CHAPTER SEVEN: RESULTS-ORIENTED TO HEARTFELT RELATIONSHIPS

When Doreen's husband, Tom, retired at age sixty-two from a senior vice president position of a Fortune 500 company, he was underfoot all the time. He started a home-based consulting business, taking over his wife's office space, computer, and telephone. Doreen had to wait until he left the house to use the computer. Her friends were unable to reach her by phone and Tom was a disaster at taking messages.

"I was shifted to second class citizenship in my own home!" Doreen lamented. "Making my telephone calls was like being in a goldfish bowl. When my friends called, he would ask 'who was that on the phone?' I found this and other intrusions to be more than a little irritating."

In retirement, men do not have a network of friends like their wives. They don't know how to include others in their lives as do women. This apparent gender inability is one of the reasons wives feel their husbands are underfoot.

RESULTS-ORIENTED VERSUS HEARTFELT RELATIONSHIPS

Work relationships are built on mutual needs and utility. Most interactions involve persons in their job roles, rather than individuals in their personal roles. Accustomed to managing many employees, we are admired and used to having people respect and carry out our decisions. We are taught not to get emotionally involved in people's lives and to refer personnel problems to the employee relations department. Employees are seen as replaceable parts in the organization, valued for their usefulness.

Outside of work, personal interactions result from conscious choice—enlivened by awareness. Since the human experience is ultimately about relationships, results-driven business people must learn to become more heartfelt. Heartfelt relationships result from deep and significant human moments.

TRANSITIONING TO HEARTFELT CONNECTIONS

Leaving the business world means leaving behind ready-made, but superficial relationships. Some relationships may endure, but many people relocate and get on with their lives.

Since maintaining deep relationships is not important in business, upon retirement relationships may be reduced to the spouse and immediate family. How do we develop significant connections?

We may find that the longest journey in life is from the head to the heart. The bumpy transition to heartfelt relationships is vividly depicted in the film, *About Schmidt.* Schmidt, an upper-level insurance company executive, retires from a firm aptly called Woodman. As an actuary, Schmidt is the classic organizational man, a wooden-like employee. In his job, he is obsessed with calculating death rates and acquires few relationship-building skills. He has a moribund marriage and his daughter resents his meddling in her life. After his wife dies, Schmidt finds it difficult to connect with people. His letters to his sponsored child from an undeveloped county reveal his feelings and self-reflections. Overcoming a self-centered, outer-directed life manipulated by external forces, he experiences a modicum of joy when he finally establishes a heartfelt connection with his overseas pen pal.

In retirement, we can be introspective and face the ultimate questions: *What's important? I've made it, but what have I made?* When we search for answers to these questions, we begin the journey from success to significance. With the journey comes the feeling of wholeness. Competition becomes less of an issue, we judge less, and we give of ourselves to reestablish our feelings of importance.

RE-CONNECTING WITH OUR PARTNERS

A deep relationship with a partner or spouse becomes the primary vehicle for learning how to develop and maintain heartfelt connections. Committed personal relationships are the safest and best places to learn about ourselves. Those closest to us become grist for the learning mill. They help us penetrate the deepest recesses of our psyches as we learn to change our behaviors.

Retirement brings a whole new dynamic to relationships. The inability of many men to downshift (give up some of their sense of importance) and relate differently to their wives creates tension. Many wives, expecting their husbands will be more relaxed, more fun, and helpful in the day-to-day interactions, are disappointed. According to one spouse, "We can't seem to communicate. He is telling me how to run the household, as though he is the boss and I'm the secretary. I wish he would get a life!" At this point, the husband feels misunderstood and unappreciated. Eventually, he will get a life and rekindle the passion, but the interim period of adjustment can be hard on relationships.

Consider the story of Beverly and Jack. Beverly's husband, Jack, was a comptroller of a Fortune 500 before he retired. He equipped his home office with a computer and second telephone line. He used the computer to manage his investment portfolio. However, that did not take all day and Jack was bored much of the time.

Beverly had a busy social schedule with several women's organizations. Soon after Jack's retirement she related, "I feel guilty going out too often and leaving him at home alone. I infrequently plan evenings out without Jack because he is home alone much of the day." While Beverly didn't openly express it, she felt an unstated righteous indignation because of his dependence on her. He was just not a lot of fun to be with these days!

Take Susan and Dean, for example. Susan had major volunteer commitments the first year Dean retired. She was reluctant to drop these activities to nurture him or to solve his problems. Although she was aware of his loneliness, restlessness, and feelings of insignificance, she allowed him to work it out. She commented, "Dean was never used to my not being at home full time that first year. Now he accepts my outside activities and his resentment is gone."

Career woman and homemaker variables. Research shows retired career women and housewives have different behaviors and emotions. Career women see themselves as having multiple roles—as retired and as homemakers—the combination leading to higher satisfaction for both husband and wife.

An increasing number of working women stay in careers long after their husbands retire, causing dynamics at home to change dramatically. Husbands of working wives are forced to accept less traditional roles in the house. With more sharing of household tasks, couples find feelings of togetherness are enhanced. Career women, unlike the housewives, don't feel the need to "baby sit" their husbands.

Homemakers, on the other hand, frequently complain about their lack of autonomy after their husbands retire. For them, the workload often becomes heavier. They fall into routines they grow to despise. With their husbands at home all the time, wives don't have any free time for themselves. They are annoyed when husbands expect them to be ready to go anywhere at the drop of a hat.

The marital dynamic between traditional couples and couples where both spouses worked is a function of the roles and responsibilities of each. The homemaker was forced to conform to her husband's schedule and availability. When both worked, each tried to accommodate the other's schedule, creating understanding and flexibility. These couples are more likely to say that retirement improved their marital relationships.

The road ahead. Retirement transition is a time of confusion, misunderstandings, and uncertainty about new responsibilities. However, stop and think about all the transitions we've navigated over a lifetime: marriage, raising and launching our children, dealing with boomerang children (those sent out of the nest who somehow found their way back home), becoming a grandparent, and coping with economic uncertainty.

Yes, there were some hurts and heartaches along the way, but we must remember the happiness associated with these times. If we're still together with our life partners, we have done lots of things well.

Realizing it took time to get to where we are today, we must allow our partners and ourselves time to adjust to this new life phase. The first step is to acknowledge and accept the reality: the rules have changed. Whatever the circumstances, each partner separately and then as a couple must define the purpose of the Wisdom Years, their respective roles, and what each wants out of the relationship. This is difficult because the possibilities and options are unlimited. These years are relatively free of obligations and careers. Starting from scratch is often a new experience, requiring both partners to reflect and rethink their belief systems.

SUPPORTIVE LOVE

Unconditional love is a difficult concept to understand, requiring some explanation. Supportive love is its practical application. Accept the premise that initially many married couples were attracted to each other because of their differences. These initially supported the division of labor and roles. When the roles dissolve in retirement, differences are magnified. Although being right and action oriented were important during the performing years, these qualities have no currency in the Wisdom Years. They will bankrupt a marriage and destroy trust and companionship.

During the career-years couples have a clear set of common goals. Raising a family and providing for financial stability are two such areas. Along with these come status, social identity, a nice house, friends and a sense of accomplishment. This changes when the last "boomerang child" finally moves out, a full-time career winds down, and the couple downsizes by moving into a condominium. With this upheaval, a new phase of life begins. What is the common goal now? What is the purpose of the relationship? The answer involves some good news and some not-so-good news.

For most of their married life, couples are joined at the hip as they "do" life together. Now it's different. The very things that brought them together, become irritants. Most couples are attracted to each other because of opposite personality characteristics. She is outgoing, he is quiet. He likes to control, she is a pleaser. You get my point. This works well as they build their life together. No money and a couple of kids are great motivators for mutual hard work that takes about 30 years. Now what do they do?

My suggestion: personal growth of the partner is the work of couples in the Wisdom Years. Supportive love is recognizing the spouse is a unique person who needs to develop whatever abilities, dreams, or creative talents have lain dormant during the career years.

Supportive love involves a new set of guidelines. Instead of being critical, judgmental, and not understanding how your partner does life, do the opposite. Encourage his/her talents and the way s/he learns. Celebrate the differences between you. Also, realize when in autopilot mode your partner is unaware. Assume his/her behavior is normal and that it's you who are out of sync with them.

Use your skills to your advantage, as in the childhood nursery rhyme: "Jack Spratt could eat no fat; his wife could eat no lean and so betwixt the two of them they licked the platter clean." Collaboration requires overcoming both ego and the fear of dependence. In a culture of a rugged individualism, there are learning opportunities when we agree with another and accept help (especially for men when their wives want to help). Supportive love transforms partners who need to prove they are right, who gather facts to lay a trap in an attempt to gain individuality, dignity, and respect.

ATTRACTING OTHERS

Transitioning to heartfelt relationships requires a significant shift in skills. An important step is to realize there is no one right answer. Each of us looks at the external world of things, interactions, people, and determines what is right from our respective points of view. It is critical we refrain from trying to change others, rather look to changing the personal view of the world we create. When we change our beliefs, we change the realities we experience.

Mahatma Gandhi's quote says it best, "You must be the change you wish to see in the world." All human life is an experiment in manifested beliefs. Whether we are Buddhist, Catholic, Fundamentalist, or Democrat or Republican, we have feedback loops reinforcing our beliefs. We are advised not to argue about two topics: politics and religion. Good advice. Contentious arguing is a zero-sum game nobody wins. When we pass judgment about who is right we only harden the other's position and retard personal growth.

An understanding of how relationships work is required. Contrary to magnets, we are repelled by people who are not like us—who don't think like us, and who do not share our beliefs. In people with opposite traits, we are able to observe personality aspects we have a hard time accepting in ourselves. We are intolerant toward others because they have the traits we disown in ourselves. We can identify aspects of ourselves by observing others. At any point in time, people will reflect our stages of personal development. Since people come in and out of our lives all the time, as we change, so do the mirror images.

These aspects represent our unconscious beliefs about people, politics, religion, and a host of ideas from societal conditioning. We can infer these beliefs exist from observing our critical behaviors. From the well-known twelve-step process, we know, "If you spot it, you got it."

Paradoxically, the more we resist owning the shadow side, the more prominent it becomes. We judge others until we realize the discontentment is about ourselves. When we resolve issues, they recede into the background and other issues come to the foreground. Without this circular reflective and reasoning process, we could not look at ourselves and know who we are.

Life is designed for companionship and intimacy. Letting go of judgment and criticism allows for creating and maintaining the heartfelt relationships so essential for personal growth.

PONDER THIS

Life is designed for companionship and intimacy. Letting go of judgment and criticism allows for creating and maintaining the heartfelt relationships essential for personal growth. Ponder the following questions to help you clarify progress in shifting from a business-like results-oriented focus to heartfelt relationships.

- Am I interacting with others as if I were still on the job?

- Are deep heartfelt connections important to me?
- Have I replaced lost business relationships with personal friends?
- Do I provide support to my significant other?
- Have I defined our respective roles, and what each wants out of the relationship?
- When interacting with others, can I listen for the intention, support without judgment, and differ against the common goal rather than argue?
- What irritates me in others? Where do I find judgment? Isn't criticism more about me than others?

CHAPTER EIGHT: FROM SUCCESS TO PERSONAL VISION

Joyce is searching for her passion. In creating and managing eight different businesses, she has learned from one enterprise to next. As she continued her business career into her fifties and sixties, no sweat. In her seventies, she has discovered she is no longer the best in the crowd. But she still wants to win. Selective about getting involved in new things, she's focusing on being a coach, not a player. She's mentoring young entrepreneurs—trying to pick winners—newcomers in business who need help.

In the Wisdom Years, we search for renewed purpose in our lives and learn to feel important by engaging in value-added activities. There are no policies and no performance requirements—and no one to do it for us.

Each of us is handed a clean slate and is responsible for filling it. We create our own happiness by managing ourselves—our beliefs, attitudes, creative capital, core competencies, and personal relationships. We ponder the significant questions: *Who am I? What are my passions? How do I use my unique talents to bring gratification to my life? Which beliefs help in this process? Which hinder*? As a result of this soul searching, we have a deeper awareness of self and the purpose of life. Through reappraisal and recommitment, we redefine our human values. When we choose activities congruent with our values, we experience the continual joy of personal growth.

Like Joyce, we spent our performing years focused on outer-driven purposes to achieve business results and economic well-being. During the journey to the Wisdom Years, another purpose takes precedence. We discover a new kind of satisfaction—a deepening sense of being-ness—experiencing the world from the inside out. We realize that genuine gratification is internal. Thus, managing retirement means managing ourselves. This inner-driven vision results in an intensified personhood.

TRANSITIONING TO A PERSONAL VISION

The search for gratification. What happens when we lose outer-driven purpose and we are bereft of the status, perks, paychecks, or personnel associated with our business careers?

Concentration camp victims are extreme examples of those stripped of everything. Yet even when enduring the horror of man's inhumanity to man, they search for meaning in life. Following his experience in the World War II death camps, Viktor E. Frankl wrote *Man's Search for Meaning*. He said, "We all had once been or had fancied ourselves to be 'somebody.' Now we were treated like complete nonentities." Stripped of clothes, personal effects, and even his name, Frankl became simply a number.

For the concentration camp survivors, there was a common theme: "a man who becomes conscious of the responsibility he bears toward another who waits for him, or to an unfinished work [in Frankl's case his handwritten notes], will never be able to throw away his life. He who knows the 'why' of his existence will be able to bear almost any 'how.' The will to meaning is the basic motivation of human life. It is this spiritual freedom—which can not be taken away—that makes life meaningful and purposeful." Frankl's personal fight to find meaning in a hostile environment is an inspiration to everyone.

In retirement, we begin the journey in search of life's meaning. This requires us to craft new visions that sustain and inspire. In examining unfamiliar aspects of ourselves, parts left undeveloped, hidden, or rejected, we discover new sources of energy, untapped wisdom, and imagination. This is the time for connecting with newfound vitality, passion, and calling. It involves re-prioritizing life interests to create a new vision.

The importance of feeling important. The lack of feeling important or useful is the root cause of disappointment in retirement. But there is no difference between being "somebody," and being "anybody." In *Managing Retirement*, Howard Shank attacked his post-career experience as a management problem needing a solution. His insight: the problem has a name and that name is *importance*.

Shank recounts the story of a bus driver who acted out his dream, retired to Florida, and took it easy. "He began to realize how important his work had been in the lives of many. He realized he had pride in his work. Nothing took its place for him. He didn't find situations in which he felt he had significance in other people's lives. He didn't try very hard. He lost his self respect and was unhappy for the remaining years he lived."

The key words are: *nothing took its place for him.* The challenge is to find something to replace being somebody—activities that provide a feeling of importance. Otherwise, we will judge every opportunity with a critical eye measured against our careers and wind up like the bus driver.

Transitioning to being just anybody and still feeling important requires an attitude adjustment. We must get over wanting to be somebody and get on with what is important to us. What is important is in the eye of the beholder, each of us. It is no longer about what people think of us. Engaging in value-added activities produces the feeling of importance.

From success to significance. When productive activity involves something larger than ourselves and is appreciated by others, we are rewarded with feelings of gratification. We seek such value satisfaction every day.

If we can say, "There is value in what I do; someone cares about what I do; what I do is significant to me and to others," we have value satisfaction. At its core, importance is uniquely personal and intrinsically rewarding. Each of us has the responsibility to search for our own uniqueness. Otherwise, there is no meaning to life.

OBSTACLES TO FINDING SATISFACTION IN LIFE

Living in the past or the future. Business is about looking in the rearview mirror to explain why things went poorly and answering the boss' question: *What are you going to do for me tomorrow?* Forty years of this conditioning teaches us to solve problems and plan future results. Only the past and the future are questioned, so we spend little time in the present. Such thinking is not effective in retirement.

People hang onto the past and keep it alive to maintain a sense of personal importance. Much of their identities are tied to what they did—schools attended, jobs held, trips taken, places lived, or houses owned. Who are you if others don't know your past?

With no purpose, no goals, no juice from a current passion, people relive the memories of what they did; it helps re-establish social identity and sense of importance.

In her classic work, *The Coming of Age*, Simone de Beauvoir explains why older people keep retrieving images from the past. "They are not trying to make a detailed, coherent account of their earlier years, but rather to plunge back into them. Repeatedly they turn over a few themes of great emotional value to them; and far from growing tired of this perpetual repetition, they return to it with even greater pleasure. They escape from the present; they dream of former happiness; they exorcise past misfortunes."

Retirees who are disillusioned and bored with nothing to anticipate, re-tell the same stories. They relive their college and fraternity days, revel in their exploits, and talk about *the good old days.* While the past is an experience platform to build on, choosing to relive the glory days has a downside. Remember, thoughts and emotions create the reality we experience. Whatever we concentrate on becomes manifest. So, be careful. By constantly retelling our stories, we may get more of the same, or disappointment if we can't do what we once did. Without purpose, there is nothing but the past.

On the other hand, anticipation of better days ahead may lead to the *silent trap of future.* Believing things will be better or worse creates anxiety. Like living in the past, living in the future is a state of non-personhood, devoid of joy. Restlessness, anxiousness, and feelings of being in a void pervade the soul. If the past gives us identity, the future promises more of what we had, but lost.

Being emotionally unprepared for the transition. Pre-retirement offers the opportunity to prepare emotionally for a major change, but this rarely happens. As a result, many new retirees experience what is similar to a midlife crisis. When we experienced a midlife crisis in our early forties we asked: *Have I made it?* or *I've made what?* If we ask these same questions now, we are reflecting on purpose. It signals a transition to another stage.

Denying the opportunity to experience a transition crisis is another of life's traps. If we didn't experience these questions in our forties, then we will eventually. It starts with a vague restlessness leading to the question: *Now what do I do?* It creeps up in subtle ways. Reduced social involvement, the loss of structure, a lack of work focus, all can bring on classic post-retirement disorientation and mild depression.

This depression may cause an inability to prioritize and handle normal daily tasks, little things, like cleaning the garage, organizing the home office, or accomplishing a "honey-do" list. When the present is without purpose and the future is without prospect, life comes to a virtual standstill. We find ourselves running in place, being dominated by activities, then new insecurities, and uncertainties. Typical of these feelings of entrapment are narrow thinking, self-absorption, a narcissistic tendency, and a *me* focus. There appears to be no way out of the funk. Everything seems to be closing in.

Loss or confusion is the price we pay for living, but they lay the foundation for growth. Eventually we are nudged to question our purposes, beliefs, and values, and—after a degree of pain and soul-searching—to arrive at unique re-definitions of who we are and what is important to us.

This is the work of the Wisdom Years. We psychologically die so there will be progress. Through personal reappraisal and recommitment, we redefine human values.

Take Bill for example. He is questioning his entire life, even his identity. He asks: Who am I? What have I accomplished? What is life all about? He has no answers. He is hurting inside and yet doesn't know why. At times, he's immobile and has trouble doing the simplest things.

There is an inconsistency in Bill's life between" what should be" and" what is." As he chases more material stuff, his inner voice questions everything. As long as he has vacations and things to collect, he has something to anticipate and discuss. The more he experiences, the more he wants. Like an addiction, if he stops, the withdrawal symptoms are unbearable. He keeps up the pace to avoid depression. Because he experiences no long-term satisfaction, the best of times is becoming the worst of times. Can he find happiness only by going through the pain of piecing together his own set of values?

The Chinese use two characters to describe the change. One is danger, the other opportunity. Danger means change, since change must occur if a crisis is to be resolved. In the personal crisis of retirement, the old rules don't work and there are no new rules. So what are we supposed to do? To find happiness, Bill must move from affluent throwaway pleasure to a deeper purpose. In retirement, we learn to define happiness in new ways.

CREATING YOUR OWN HAPPINESS

We receive the torch of life and pass on our unique flames as individuals, families, communities, and cultures. This evolutionary process strengthens the spiritual fiber of society. Bible study groups and religious books probe life's meaning. Self-help books suggest we look within, at our own wants and dreams. In his book, *Purpose-Driven Life: What on Earth Am I Here For?* Rick Warren believes the starting place must be with the Divine—and the eternal purpose of each life.

A life of significance has its rewards, whether it's living in a monastery, sitting on a hilltop reflecting, or as George Burns put it, "having a good meal, a good cigar, and a good woman. Or a bad woman depending on how much happiness you can stand."

Martin Seligman is no George Burns, but provides a researcher's view of happiness in *Authentic Happiness*. His observations correlate with anecdotal evidence. First, there is no one path to happiness. "Lasting satisfaction comes not from money, status, or fleeting pleasure, but from rising to the challenge of deep relationships and activities tied to a clear purpose in life. Life circumstance has little to do with satisfaction. Health, wealth, good looks, and status have astonishing little effect on what researchers call *subjective well-being*." Seligman reports paraplegics and lottery winners typically return to their personality norms once they have had six months to adjust to their sudden change in fortune.

These findings are consistent with Sheehy's study showing that happiness has little to do with business-oriented variables, such as previous title, degree of success or failure, current net worth, and amount of work in post retirement.

George Vaillant drew similar conclusions from his *Aging Well* study. Where we grew up, how much money our parents made, where we went to school, "parental social class, stability of parental marriage, parental death in childhood, family cohesion, and IQ [of the parents]" were not predictive factors of being happy.

Results of these three studies show one significant variable: the people who enjoyed the highest well-being reached out for new gratifying adventures and developed fulfilling personal relationships. They viewed retirement as an opportunity to add depth, meaning, and richness to their lives. Conquering the longing for meaning is one of the most important factors in controlling a retiree's outlook on life. Unhappy retirees have done nothing productive beyond pleasing themselves.

Another significant variable is mature love. Sheehy found that ninety percent of the happiest men were in love with their wives and close to their children. In contrast, only half of the unhappiest men were close to their spouse and children. Similarly, Seligman found the happiest couples were not the most realistic, but the most positive. They idealized their partners and predicted their relationships would withstand hard times."

Attitude is everything. Sure, *attitude is everything*, but how do we define it? Attitude is inner-directed—desiring to do things with people and loving with empathy. It's about knowing ourselves well. Identity surges from the *inside out* and people know the person inside.

In a practical sense, attitude is the by-product of identifying and using the creative talents and traits we possess and calling upon these in good and bad times. Building on strengths, we engage in gratifying activities. Feeling satisfaction, we project positive attitudes. Many clichés describe attitude: seeing the glass as half-full, making lemonade out of lemons, or realizing that pleasure and pain are but two sides of the same coin—so don't sweat life.

"Don't sweat it," we say, but what about adversity and suffering? There is so much pain in the world. This is true, but hardships have more to do with how we respond to life than how life deals with us. Hopeful optimism is the antidote when bad events strike. Hope has its foundation in the belief that there are permanent and universal causes for good. Optimism results from applying our signature strengths and is key in rebuilding hope.

Some people believe there is no purpose to human experience. Others are bound to their religious beliefs. It is important to realize how beliefs determine reality:

Your beliefs color what you absorb from life's experiences. What you see, the reality you create, and the outcomes you experience are directly tied to your beliefs: thoughts, past conditioning, and expectations. Your beliefs look one hundred percent correct to you and other viewpoints, including those in this book, are suspect.

If you have a vague feeling that retirement could and should be more gratifying, then you will be, *open to everything* and attached to *nothing*. This is the best way to ensure in the Wisdom Years that your life is authentically you.

TRY THIS

The following four exercises require you to think deeply about what is productive and effective use of your remaining years, concluding with a suggestion to articulate your personal vision and explain it to those close to you:

- verify your preparedness
- highpoints in your life
- your likes and dislikes
- the purpose of your life

Transitioning from business success to personal significance requires a vision. Realizing an ample third of life is left, what is the purpose of the next stage? What needs pursuit? What is to be mastered? If continued growth is your destiny, what do you want grow into?

Verify your preparedness. Growth is like negotiating a long stairway. With a burst of energy and development, we climb to new heights, only to stop and rest a while and plateau, to integrate what we have learned while preparing to take the next step. To verify your preparedness for the Wisdom Years, think about or better yet jot down your answers to these six questions.

- Do the Wisdom Years need a defined purpose? Why or why not?
- Can you describe your talents, personal strengths, and special qualities?
- Do you recognize how the pattern of your life events has reflected a life purpose? What is it? Name it and claim it. Some might label it "your calling."
- From these, can you identify your most passionate activities? Are you doing them?
- Do you have supportive love from others to follow your life purpose?

Highpoints in your life. You need to live your life backwards in this exercise. Find a clean sheet of paper and write at the top "Highpoints in My Life." Then, create these categories in a vertical column on the left side of the page: 60 to 70; 50 to 60; 40 to 50; 30 to 40; 20 to 30; < 20. Now go back over your life and relive the highpoints for each age. For each, ask yourself these questions:

- What gave you the greatest satisfaction?
- What was gratifying in your career?
- When were you successful? What were you doing?

- Even if they hadn't paid you, would you still be willing to do the work?
- In college or in the early years what subjects turned you on?
- What were your early creative abilities? Do you still enjoy them?

Assume you are applying for the ideal job. What would you tell the person interviewing about what you want to do?

Your conclusion: What is the common thread that runs through the highpoints in your life? Capture this insight by writing it down so you can share it with someone else.

Your likes and dislikes. The purpose of the following exercise is to build on your creative strengths and minimize the effects of your fears. At the top of a new sheet of paper write "Likes." Quickly list everything you like to do. What makes you happy? What comes easily for you? Include hobbies, aspects from your work experience, sports, social situations, your favorite pastime, your favorite hangouts, even pleasurable sensations.

Refer to the previous exercise and the things that gave you joy and satisfaction. List a minimum of fourteen items, those that give you pleasure or a sense of bliss. Don't over-analyze this exercise; write down whatever pops into your mind. If you think, "No I shouldn't say that," write it down anyway. This is your list and no one will see it. If you want to include more items, do so.

Next, from your list select the three or four items you enjoy most, are fun, and give you pleasure. They must be *creative* endeavors requiring you to use your unique talents. When you are engaged in these activities time flies and you get an afterglow of satisfaction.

Now answer these two questions: Are you having fun? Moreover, do you see a correlation between creativity and your strengths?

At the top of the next page write the word "Dislikes." These are things you don't like to do. List anything in which you have limited skills, you find hard to do, or that makes you feel uncomfortable. This list may be harder to construct. Recall situations where you tried to control an unpleasant environment or where you avoided confrontation and conflict. Detail activities you would not normally do, but agree to do to please someone else. Again, don't over-analyze this exercise. Write down whatever comes to mind.

Now look at this list. Circle three or four items that cause you uncomfortable feelings, avoidance, or underlying fear. These may be part of your core being or may come from past hurts and disappointments. After you have completed this exercise, return to this page and read the next paragraph about fears.

Most fears can be classified as control or approval issues. Managers, for example, who are reluctant to delegate, fear the loss of control and "not looking good" if there is a screw-up. For example, avoiding rejection and seeking approval are positive drivers for many salespeople. Wanting our children's acceptance may play into an over-giving behavior. There is some of each in us, but one characteristic dominates.

Typically, your spouse is one way and you are the other. Ask your spouse about your normal tendency. Do you typically seek approval or do you fear the loss of control? These barriers can hold you back in your personal growth.

The purpose of your life. In *Authentic Happiness*, Seligman states, "If you find yourself stuck in the parking lot of [retirement] life, with few and only ephemeral pleasures, with minimal gratification, and without meaning, there is a road out. This road takes you through the countryside of pleasure and gratification, up into the high country of strength and virtue, and finally to the peaks of lasting fulfillment, meaning, and purpose."

To authenticate a gratifying life, complete the next activity. Answer "Yes" or "No" to each statement. Add up the number of "Yes" responses and divide by ten. This will give you a percentage. If you scored in the seventieth or eightieth percentile, you are ready for the last exercise. If not, what aspects don't make sense? Reread the applicable book sections again, and then proceed to the last exercise.

- I know what values really matter in my life.
- I think about whether I am living the life I want to lead.
- I do not let the unknown shape my destiny.
- I keep my vision in mind when making important decisions.

- I understand and acknowledge my life path.
- I have a plan for how I want to live my life.
- Even people who do not know me well can tell what matters to me.
- Introspection about the meaning of my life is a valuable use of time.
- I have a clear vision of my purpose in life.
- The way I spend most of my days reflects my purpose.

Choice is the one thing that cannot be taken away from us. It is what makes life purposeful. Life provides us beauty, art, nature and the opportunity to experience pleasure in creative activities. But another aspect of life, independent of both pleasure and gratification, is an attitude about life itself.

Your personal vision. On your last sheet of paper, write "My Personal Vision." Make sure you are in a quiet place where you will not be interrupted. Sit in a comfortable chair and go within, or just close your eyes. Ask yourself, "What is my purpose in life?" "Why am I here?" Repeat those questions slowly and listen. You have the answers. Your inner voice will tell you. No fireworks, no ego, just a hint of an answer. Whatever comes to mind, capture the insight. Don't analyze anything yet.

Before going to bed, put the statement by your bedside and ask the same questions. If you have an early morning epiphany, write it down. It is elusive and will evaporate if you do not capture it. Having done the preliminary work from the previous exercises, you will find the answers are forthcoming.

What is your conclusion? To validate your vision, to make it real and authentic to you, explain it to someone close to you. Do they get it? From their perspective, is it you? Now that you have articulated your vision, you are ready to live in the precious present and realize your authentic self.

PONDER THIS

Before leaving this chapter, ask yourself the following questions:

- What am I doing here in the first place?
- Am I maximizing my gifts and talents?

CHAPTER NINE: POSITION POWER TO PERSONAL POWER

When Nell's husband, Greg, retired from a large aerospace agency, she was still working. Greg became a consulting engineer involved in experimental manufacturing projects. But he failed to adjust to the fact that his previous secretary had handled all of his personal affairs. After several utility companies cut service to the house because of missed payments, Nell felt she had to retire. She needed to take on the role of Greg's secretary to handle their personal finances and the administrative tasks of his new business. She said, "He was like an absent minded professor, out to lunch and totally inept at handling details!"

We know men and women communicate differently. Women like to talk and express their feelings and emotions without seeking solutions to problems. They just want someone to listen.

Men, on the other hand, having spent a lifetime solving problems, respond to expressions of frustration with an endless array of suggestions. They revert to the Mr. Fix It mode. Used to having "position power," they suggest or insist, there is a better way to do things, like organize the kitchen. Such behavior can result in an unpleasant power struggle. Whereas he insists he's only trying to help, she sees it as meddling in her world…and perhaps mutters under her breath "get a life."

In the workplace, position power is associated with a variety of factors. The management hierarchy is an example, where position power is equated to the total number of people you manage, your sphere of influence, and the physical proximity of your desk to the boss. Even the executive secretary wields considerable power, controlling not only the calendar, but who gets access.

Technical experts have position power. So do professionals, such as doctors, lawyers, engineers, and accountants, who wield considerable power due to their special expertise. Leaders, such as politicians, the clergy, salespeople, and lobbyists have influence power.

In retirement, we may try to maintain a false sense of importance from position power, since its loss is a blow to the ego. The resulting void of insignificance screams to be filled. If personal power is undeveloped, there is an ongoing need to be in control, to be right, to win, and to be viewed as superior. In this struggle, relying on what worked in the past is an attempt to maintain position power.

Remember this powerful prayer: God grant me the serenity to accept the things I cannot change, courage to change the things I can, and wisdom to know the difference.

Consider this shocking advice. Stop trying to control what you can't. What goes on in the world "out there" is out of your control. Your skills of controlling and directing people in the material world will not work in the Wisdom Years.

The only thing you have control over is yourself—meaning your beliefs. Your future will be a reflection of your present-day beliefs unless replaced by new ones. If you are not content with your post career life—relationships, health, interests, or spiritual tranquility—you will want to replace legacy beliefs behavior patterns with new ones. Your thoughts, beliefs, and attitudes about life—all the thoughts in your personal database—need close inspection. The focus now is you—your personal power.

The precious present. We are taught that we are at the mercy of our experiences, so we examine the past, looking for the source of personal difficulty. But we're not at the mercy of the past unless we believe we are. A focus on the past just requires more time on a psychiatrist's couch. When we focus on what is wrong, we block what is a possible.

Our point of power is the present. We are able to rid ourselves of legacy beliefs by re-patterning in the present. We use the past as a rich source of information. Rather than focus on the negative, our job is to sift through our beliefs and identify success patterns.

PERSONAL POWER

Intention. The first step in developing personal power is to realize that **the present is your point of power.** Forget about the past and the "what ifs" of the future. If you assign greater focus to the past, you will feel ineffective and deny yourself the power of the present. If you live in the future, hope will turn to anxiety and leave you drained. The only point of effective action is in the ***now.***

Present intention governs future events. Everything in the universe has the foundation of intention. The intention to grow and realize full potential is the most fundamental intention. Humans can tap into the vibrating spiritual energy field of intention to learn about personal power and create heartfelt connections.

J.W. Goethe wrote: "Until one is committed, there is hesitancy, the chance to draw back, always ineffectiveness. Concerning all acts of initiative (and creation), there is one elementary truth - the ignorance of which kills countless ideas and splendid plans; that the moment one definitely commits oneself, then Providence moves, too. All sorts of things occur to help one that would never otherwise have occurred. A whole stream of events issues from the decision, raising in one's favor all manner of unforeseen incidents and meetings and material assistance, which no man could have dreamed would have come his way. Whatever you can do, or dream you can, begin it. Boldness has genius, power, and magic in it. Begin it now."

Goethe's truth-seeking approach reflects the power of universal energy, which aligns with intention, turning thoughts into things without the need to control the outcome. It requires you to visualize your positive intentions and let them unfold without specifying how they will happen. This is difficult to put into practice, since it runs counter to work experience, where results happen from directives and task assignments. How can you move toward this goal? Through self-observation.

Self–observation. Self-observation is crucial for developing personal power. It allows for critical awareness of what you think, say, and do—and the associated consequences. It keeps you grounded in the now, giving attention to autopilot behaviors and the link between beliefs and experienced reality.

Self-observation requires an understanding of the role the mind plays. The key is to become aware of the emotional content of our stream of conscious, but also of the one who observes, or "the silent watcher." This is how Eckhart Tolle describes personal power in his book *The Power of Now.* It is important to understand that the mind works in three major ways: reactively, analytically, and with awareness.

The **reactive mind** governs physical survival. It is the animal mind. The caveman part of the brain is still wired to defend against losses. A sudden change, like forced retirement, threatens us. This produces resistance and denial. Survival reactions are involuntary and produce strong emotions, triggering protective action. Behind all reactive emotion is an adrenal rush, providing the juice for action. For example, when the brake lights appear on the car in front, you don't stop to think, you react. This is an autopilot-survival reaction.

This same emotional juice reinforces unproductive behavior when survival is not an issue. Vindictive behavior feels justified.

Judgment feels warranted. Hate feels defensible. We automatically withdraw from pain and seek pleasure without thinking. Since these reactive reflexes take merely 1/10,000 of a second, they are difficult to short-circuit in the moment. When the mind is in reactive mode producing autopilot behaviors, personal awareness suffers.

How do you get a handle on the reactive mind? By noticing your thoughts. Often thoughts are random and confused—arising out of associations—and you don't even notice. For instance, the word "Paris" reminds me of food, which in turn reminds me of an airport, and then my last trip abroad, and so on. This is tangential thinking. We may be aware of our emotions and feelings at the moment, but we are conscious rather than self-conscious. We must look at our thoughts in a rational way.

The **analytical mind** builds knowledge—the ability to recognize cause and effect, to solve problems, and to create innovations. It's the basis of all science and the foundation of the material world. We can see how feelings turned into emotions are caused by unconscious beliefs, but it takes us only so far.

Unfortunately, the analytical mind takes on a life of its own. " I think therefore I am" reinforces the belief that I am my mind. This leads to survival defenses protecting the falsely created self. Further, the analytical mind cannot explain the mystery of life, since the spirit is not matter and is not quantifiable.

The **aware mind** understands the spirit. It responds, instead of reacting, relying on discernment rather than thinking. Memory interprets the world in light of parental conditioning, the environment, education, and personal experiences. When the mind interprets the same scenes through awareness, it is possible to set judgment aside. Awareness is unprompted and silent, rather than analyzing. It reflects a different set of assumptions. In the *Power of Now,* Tolle suggests that when the aware mind starts "watching the thinker," a higher level of consciousness becomes activated and personal power is born.

Awareness is universal and loves unconditionally. It sees the brighter side of life, making for an emotionally positive person. Such a person says, "With all the suffering, drudgery, and broken dreams, it's still a beautiful world." The happy person reflects a set of attitudes rather than a set of circumstances.

The aware mind sees the whole picture, accepting human experience and the world philosophically. It is concerned with the deeper meaning of life. While the rational mind judges good or evil, the aware mind knows such a judgment represents a natural human flaw—reflecting the individual. An aware mind is essential for understanding the Wisdom Years.

The good news about aging. When physical senses fade, we are forced to pay increased attention to what we are doing, and more importantly, why. For example when cycling, I need to pay more attention. Competitiveness is one of my egocentric behaviors. When another cyclist passes me, I react like a greyhound. My competitive juices jolt me into action. I jump on the back wheel to keep up. My honor is at stake; my performer self is challenged. Believe me, this is not the way to smell the roses. Lately, I have been anticipating this behavior and I catch myself when reacting. The time lag between my reaction and coming to my senses gets shorter and shorter. This keeps me centered in the precious present and free to choose new behavior.

When the aware mind is engaged, it is alert to the connection between emotions and an underlying belief—in my case, to prove myself. As more emotional connections are revealed, we become free of the past, free to choose different outcomes. So, wisdom suggests that we need to condition ourselves to be in the moment.

It is true that being thrown into the abyss of insignificance shatters many of our preconceived ideas about *who*, or better yet, *what* we are. When we relearn, renew, and reclaim, the aware mind comes into clear focus. It urges us to understand the meaning of personal power. As introspection replaces autopilot behaviors, we need one additional aspect: optimism.

Optimism. A person with personal power feels optimistic most of the time. Optimism is a choice—not an inheritance. It is the ability to look at any negative and respond with either a positive or a pessimistic attitude. Positive thoughts produce positive results; conversely, negative thoughts produce negative results. As W. Clement Stone, the multimillionaire and early sage of the twentieth century advised, "Make an irreversible, irrevocable, and irretrievable commitment to keep a positive mental attitude towards setbacks, problems, failures, and losses." Dr. Norman Vincent Peale's best-seller, *The Power of Positive Thinking* has the same theme—thoughts determine outcome.

If you have a positive attitude, you see few of life's challenges as overwhelming. You believe your lifestyle choices—healthy eating, regular exercise, and avoiding dangerous habits— can affect your health, energy level, and vitality. Indeed, you take pleasure in managing your life through your choices, while understanding there are no guarantees.

THE CURSE OF JUDGMENT

Judgment is an egocentric land mine that can trip us up and reduce personal power. At its core, judgment involves four aspects that can cause us to stumble.

My expectation of you. The cause of most unfulfilled expectations is a belief about how others should "do life." For example, unfulfilled expectations of a spouse or an adult child can turn into critical judgments. Beliefs about expectations, underlie much of the frustration and anger between couples. Because spouses experience life differently, their expectations often are not in their consciousness. In cases where parents had children late in life, adult children are getting started just when parents are retiring. If expectations of adult children do not materialize, parents are upset.

I have a trait I do not like and I see it in you. Going a little deeper, we find ourselves criticizing others if we see behaviors we consciously or unconsciously do not like in ourselves or would never do. Let's say someone cuts me off on the freeway. I comment, "I wouldn't do that."

We judge others by our own values, but they are operating on theirs—which they believe are valid. During the formative years, children learn the best and the worst from their parents. Young adult children are critical of parents for the same trait they, themselves, possess.

Now turn the tables. Do you see in your children traits you find uncomfortable? If so, chances are you have the same trait. Children often mirror our own traits.

What I deny in myself and see in you. When denial is involved, it is almost impossible to recognize judgment. Take my attitude about money for example, traceable to my childhood. I believed that people who made lots of money were greedy; that there was something wrong with making money, that such people were unhappy and snobbish. I criticized them because it was an uncomfortable side of myself. Fortunately, I've replaced these beliefs about money with other more positive ones.

Denial works this way: We are critical of behaviors we deny in ourselves, yet see in others. Denial recognizes the trait in others and justifies judgments and righteousness.

You have something I admire and want. Desiring something others possess can result in judgment. For example, yearning for a new car might result in derogatory remarks toward people with new cars. We may not understand our behaviors at the time and feel justified, even righteous in the criticism. The desire may be related to talents or abilities, that we feign we do not want. When we deny our desires, we may rationalize our frustrations by making judgments.

LIFE'S TENSION PARADOXES

Life's real work is about dealing with choices and finding wholeness. The major obstacle in achieving oneness is tension between people caused by judgment. In marriage for example, the relationship is seldom free of the struggle to preserve power.

Opposing viewpoints are deep beliefs established through acculturation. They color thinking, determine behavior, and create ongoing conflict. Even though they run our lives, opposing viewpoints are difficult to recognize and even harder to accept as merely opinions.

Life is full of opposite viewpoints and positions—and all sides are true. Opposites are linear gradations along an arbitrary scale of measurement. Polarity is a convenient way of describing the extremes—the absence or presence of entities. Darkness is the absence of light. Evil does not exist; rather it is the absence of good. Cold and hot are gradations of temperature and are subject to opinion.

The familiar male-female conflict is a classic example. Duality, so the myth goes, was created in the Garden of Eden when Eve tempted Adam with fruit from the tree of good and evil. When he ate the apple, they were forced to leave the garden of timeless unity for an earthly experience. Symbolically, they were forced to experience separation to find their way back home. Dating from creation, polarity is the source of human conflict and the roadblock to wisdom.

We must be careful not to extend duality irrationally. For example, good is not necessarily balanced by evil. Nor does evil exist to show the way to good. If you believe that you were born a sinner and that goodness must be redeemed, your personal accountability is compromised, and you are at fate's mercy. Such thoughts can cause great torment and suffering.

Realize, if all opposite forces suddenly ceased to exist, free will would not be needed and human civilization, as we know it, would not exist. There would be no need for a material world, no learning, and no evolution of the human spirit. Without the cycles of good and bad luck, pain and pleasure, risk and reward, and health and illness, life would be devoid of meaning and joy. There would be no challenge, no personal growth, and no movement of civilization. Life would be without learning.

As discussed above, judgment is an obstacle to learning—yet, it is the human condition to find fault in how others view the world. They cannot be right if I am right. So couples argue with each other, nations fight for their truths, and political parties sling mud. Being in the world, but not of it requires detachment; letting others live their life by withholding judgment. It is the basis of religious freedom. Learning life's lessons is a personal experience and all of human history relates to this learning. It is the ongoing process of a soul's purification on the way to self-realization and understanding the Absolute Spirit—the unity and oneness in everything.

UNITY AND ONENESS

There is a unifying force within us—a desire is to become whole—to identify with the Source of our creation. When we rise against adversity, we glimpse a sense of enduring validity not deigned. It is the core of being human and the basis of personal power.

Everything flows from a cosmic consciousness—the Source of all things. Source exists independently of all intellectual or sensory perception of it. The intention of a consciousness, human or divine, is creative growth. Although consciousness evolves on an earthly plane through evolution, it is sourced from above, like sunlight pouring energy into the Earth to sustain life, from the simplest to the most complex forms. Through enlightenment, man is destined to return to the Source of life itself.

We are in life's classroom, learning to resolve the tensions and return to the garden of timeless unity and our Source. Continuing with the Adam and Eve parable, the schism occurred so they would search for and be reunited with God. Myth has it that sexual union allowed each to experience God. Physical union may be a tentative link to experiencing the divine, yet it is a start. Resolving male-female tension is a powerful learning experience. Compassion, reserving judgment, relinquishing control, and supporting one another is part of maturation and wisdom.

Either/or thinking prevents the possibility of oneness. From the tension of opposing pairs, we realize a third alternative—a middle ground. It does not deny the validity of either polarity, but requires withholding judgment. Creativity results from the tension between spontaneity and limitations.

The trick is to position yourself in the middle of opposite pairs and acknowledge that both extremes exist simultaneously. It means experiencing the highs and lows of life and acknowledging the capacity to create good and bad outcomes.

Opposites create the tensions we are constantly forced to resolve. Out of such resolution comes progress and evolution. The speed at which we get conflict under control is the degree to which we understand life's work. When we acknowledge that such tensions result in personal growth, adversity becomes a positive experience.

This quote from Wayne Dyer's book, *The Power of Intention* sums up this topic. His question: Which are you? "Matter or absence? The physical or metaphysical? Form or spirit? The answer is both, even though they appear to be opposites. Do you have a free will, and are you part of the destiny of intention? Yes. Fuse the dichotomy. Blend the opposite, and live with both of these beliefs. Begin the process of allowing Spirit to work with you, and link up to the field of intention."

Purification of the earthly soul. I use the term *purification of the soul* to describe the process of reconciling differences. The German philosopher Hegel interprets all of human history as a progressive self-realization toward the Absolute Spirit. For him, self-realization is the spiritual progress behind all human history. Thus, the role of man is to see Spirit realizing itself in the world.

Creative tension is the vehicle for this opportunity. Tensions from duality provide for interaction, cooperation, or conflict—and lead to personal growth.

TRY THIS

Stop planning. Forget the traditional ways business gets results. In the performing years the admonition was "Don't just sit there; do something." Better, faster, more, and improved productivity were the measures of success. When reconnecting to your authentic self, business approaches are ineffective for the evolving you. Unless aware of this fact, you'll get more of the same plus frustration. Unless there is a fundamental shift, "you will always get what you always got" and wonder why life isn't working.

Looking back, I realize most of my life was an autopilot response. I was reactive, and with sheer force and a rational approach, got results and success followed. Only recently, I've become more aware. Now before judging another person, I stop, reflect, and realize the judgment is about me, not them. I'm learning how to act rather than react. Listening to what others have to say, and not jumping to a preconceived idea of what they're saying, slows down my reactiveness. I'm applying the carpenter's advice: measure twice and cut once. Awareness is about consequences.

Develop personal power through clear intentions. With an aware mind, optimism in dealing with adversity, and clear intentions define personal power. It all starts with intention. These are mine:

- I intend to use my aware mind to be optimistic, no matter what life throws at me.
- I intend to be healthy, fit, and sustain a pleasurable life with all my senses intact.
- I intend to develop to their fullest potential my God-given talents enjoying the gratification they bring me and others.
- I intend to experience heartfelt connections with family and friends to express my love and feelings of fulfillment.
- I intend to continue to grow as a spiritual being to have meaning in my life.

Notice how each statement is a choice about how I want to be. The word "choose" can replace the word "intend." In either case, when you vividly visualize a desire and associate emotional feelings with it, as Goethe's quote suggests, the universe supports your commitment in mysterious ways.

Identify a personal philosophy. Each of us has the opportunity to develop spiritually after birth, experiencing the soul's desire. To achieve this ideal, we need a personal philosophy that integrates the practical and metaphysical. In resolving conflicts and understanding our personal responsibility in creating illness, pain, and suffering, we purify our souls. Like a monk on a mountaintop reflecting, ask yourself:

- I've made it, I've made what?
- I've done it, I've done what?

Take the monk's reflective approach and answer these questions for yourself. Describe your personal power. What aspects of position power have you shed to uncover it? Share these insights with a significant other. Do they get it? If there is duality, e.g. the male-female dance, describe your approach for reducing conflict and encouraging collaboration.

PONDER THIS

Before leaving this chapter, ask yourself the following questions:

- Why is personal power never connected with what's "out there?"
- Why is our "point of power" in the present—not in the past or future?

CHAPTER TEN: THE FOUR ESSENTIAL INGREDIENTS IN LIFE

Two themes run through this book. The first theme: love and gratitude provide purpose and meaning in life. Love is the active energy of giving oneself unconditionally to another and providing support. By contrast, gratitude is passive energy, a positive expression acknowledging the gift of life, with all it entails on a personal level. Quoting Viktor Frankl, “A man who becomes conscious of the responsibility he bears toward another who waits for him (love), or to an unfinished work, (gratitude) will never be able to throw away his life.”

The second theme: beliefs shape reality. Beliefs are best understood from this statement: “Change the belief and what I experience changes.”

Life after full-time work is an undefined journey to the Wisdom Years. No two paths are the same. Introspection and discovery are the currency.

During the Wisdom Years, we stop to reflect about what makes life valuable and consider four crucial components: 1) renewed *pleasure* from physical well-being, 2) *gratification* from using the intellect to engage in creative activities, 3) heartfelt *fulfillment* from interacting with others, and 4) *meaning* from making a spiritual connection. A balance of these four essential ingredients creates happiness.

THE PLEASURABLE LIFE OF PHYSICAL SENSATIONS

Most of us equate happiness with pleasure. A hot shower, a great glass of merlot, a Marine band playing the Star-Spangled Banner, a beautifully restored wooden sailboat, my granddaughter's hand as it grabs onto mine—these are delights. They have clear sensory and strong emotional components requiring little thinking. These are what philosophers call the "raw feels." Other pleasurable sensations are tied to emotions, for example, a budding romance, a deal about to close, being "somebody," having people look up to you, and scoring a hole in one.

Because the capacity for pleasure is limited and not sustaining, it's hard to build a life around these sensations—even though some try. In retirement, pleasure loses its luster and leisure becomes work if too much is tied to physical stimulation.

By adapting to ever-richer indulgences, we only narrow our options for pleasing ourselves. For example, the next vacation has to top the last one to ensure a pleasurable experience. A compliment feels good, but one is not enough. After one glass of wine, I want another, the same with a handful of peanuts. To get the same high, the dosage has to increase. This includes alcohol and other addictive entities. Too much alcohol, known by retirees as sundowners disease, produces a nasty after-effect. One way to relieve the symptoms is to drink "the hair of the dog that bit you," the next day. This leads to an addictive cycle where more of the same doesn't produce greater pleasure.

Great pleasure comes from physical exercise. Whether it's walking or a game of golf, engaging in muscle movement feels good. Movement gets the heart pumping and the blood flowing. *Younger Next Year* is an excellent book advocating how staying in shape adds immeasurably to a pleasurable life.

Using your aware mind, make it a practice to purposefully engage and heighten all five senses. Periodically feel the wind on your face, smell the scent of a flower, taste the different flavors the next time you eat a meal. As you take a walk, listen to the sounds of life around you—observe nature's incredible beauty. Your point of power is being an objective observer.

However, any illness or injury can quickly snatch away this major pleasure. If we are unable to enjoy the weekly games of golf or tennis with our friends, it can be depressing. To experience yet another loss on top of career losses can be devastating. Preventative measures—maintaining a healthy lifestyle—are key.

THE FULFILLING LIFE OF HEARTFELT RELATIONSHIPS

Feeling full of life is one of life's goals. But even after a certain threshold of physical pleasure and security, more of the same does not increase fulfillment.

Fulfillment is about the heart and humans require heartfelt connections. You can have all the money in the world and everything you ever wanted. But if you are by yourself, you may be the saddest and loneliest person on the planet. Nothing money can buy will fulfill the soul's need for human contact.

Study after study confirms that a person's happiness is affected much less by income than by marital status and spirituality. We understand this when we stop and ask the question: What is it all about? Part of the answer is transitioning from hubris to humility, experiencing the fulfillment from sharing heartfelt connections with those closest to us.

Humanity is based on individual interactions, each of us creating moments of intimacy. Be present by using your personal power to stay in the moment. The goal is to dis-identify from the analytical mind and become an objective observer of the ego's need to judge. This requires you to be engaged, yet detached. The moment judgment stops, you have made room for love and heartfelt connections.

The will for meaning is the compelling force of a fulfilled life.

THE GRATIFYING LIFE OF CREATIVE EXPRESSION

While a good life is often associated with pleasure, it has a much larger component. Beyond pleasure, lies gratification, the enduring satisfaction from putting strengths to positive use in service to others. It is a transition from success to significance. The word *passion* is often associated with the creative process, reflecting intensity, focus, and involvement. The reward from creative activity is a feeling of satisfaction that resonates to the spiritual core.

When we apply our talents intensely, we experience a flow, where gratification lasts longer than pleasure. It's a feeling of being productive and doing something well. Because we are totally absorbed, it feels like time flies—we experience the essence of creative personal power. We sense the *sweet spot* in the activity and feel rewarded. We have neither thought nor feeling—we are simply one with the music we are making.

THE MEANINGFUL LIFE OF SPIRITUAL INSIGHT

Pleasure, gratification, and fulfillment are all about me. They provide a foundation for enjoying life, but they don't add to the quality of life. Nor do they increase the intensity of life's flame as the torch is passed on.

With a bountiful thirty percent of our life available in the Wisdom Years, we must answer the question: What is the purpose of life at this stage? We have a lot of time to reflect on this philosophical and spiritual question. At the core, deep within each of us, there is an internal longing to live a life of value—to really matter, to make a difference. It's leaving a legacy—leaving this world a better place.

A meaningful life combines pleasure, gratification, fulfillment, and one more ingredient—the spiritual meaning of human existence. It answers the question: Why are we here? A meaningful life is a blend of inner-directedness and other-directedness. To achieve this ideal, we use our unique talents in support of others. We follow a personal calling in life, leading to the authentic self.

Each of us has a responsibility to contribute to something larger than ourselves. It doesn't necessarily mean demonstrating for peace. Perhaps it is ensuring peace in our own families and in our interactions with others. Use the power of now and set your intention. Present intention governs future events. Everything in the universe has the foundation of intention. To grow and realize full potential is the most fundamental intention. Through intention, we tap into the vibrating spiritual energy field of intention to create a life of meaning. A meaningful life is uplifting to the human spirit and contributes a human moment.

MEASURING SUCCESS AT EACH STAGE

Each stage of life has a purpose. Looking back, we ask: Was I effective? Was I productive? Did I do the right things? In the learning years, we measure by grades and adopting society's values. In the performing years, we use economic stability and social identity as the yardstick. In the Wisdom Years, we point to our heartfelt connections, expressions of core competencies, and contributions beyond self-pleasure. The essence is not the positions we have held, but who we are as individuals.

Transitioning between life's stages. When a formal career ends, a new phase of life begins—the goal of which is wisdom. We must break away from societal conditioning and the falsely created self to rediscover individual originality and authenticity.

In redefining personal power, we begin to understand the meaning of life. Life's insights are often elusive if we cling to what we did, our social identity, and the illusion of youth. A famous psychologist said that it is impossible to live in the evening of life using midday rules. What had great importance then, will have little now. Further, the truth of the morning will also be the error of the evening.

As we leave our career years, there is a pressing need to understand what's next. To grow, we need to be more introspective and meditative. To win at retirement, we need to become more personal, to become more heartfelt, and to develop our personal power. In the summer of our lives, we reached outside; now in the autumn years, we must seek from within.

We create our own realities. We are not held prisoner by retirement or the past. Somewhere, on a porch or by a lake, a retired person divides his/her time between grandchildren, exercising, fly-fishing, travel, projects involving his/her passion, and continued spiritual development. Through conscious choice, s/he has created a personal reality. The retirement experience is the result of the choices each of us makes.

During one of our interviews, one executive said it best:

"To me retirement is a little bit like the sound barrier that Chuck Yeager broke. People were scared to death of it and they didn't know if the plane would crumble and blow up; they didn't know what would happen. It turned out that nothing happened. They passed right through it. All kinds of things were then enabled when they were on the other side of that imagined barrier. And that's how retirement is."

All kinds of possibilities open up once you get through it. All of a sudden you're free to do so many things you desire. It's an enormous, empowering feeling to say, "It's up to me. What I make out of the rest of my life is up to me."

PONDER THIS

Before leaving this chapter, ask yourself the following questions:

- Why keep my body in motion?
- Why connect with others?
- Why have a purpose?
- Why have a spiritual quest?
- How can I create balance of all four aspects of my life?

ACKNOWLEDGMENTS

I would like to acknowledge Patricia Benesh, of AuthorAssist for clarifying the complex psychological and emotional issues of retirement to ensure readability. Patricia, you take concepts, ideas, and disjointed thoughts and make them sing. I am deeply grateful for your support. Becky Avera and Debbie Butcher, thank you for your proofing skills and being members of the team.

To Jeanne Little, who interviewed countless wives of retired husbands, creating an original chapter entitled "The Wives Speak," thank you for your research efforts. Those invaluable vignettes now are sprinkled throughout the book.

As I learn from Heather Lawn, Grant Powers, and Dean Wickstrom, I continually enhance my understanding of the nature of personal reality. I value your encouragement throughout the years.

The personal stories and frustrations shared by many men and women form the content backbone. Like them, I have experienced the ups and downs of life after full-time work. Thank you to these individuals and to my friends and colleagues who read long, initial drafts. Your insights and suggestions helped shape a viable book.

Love and gratitude to Mary, my wife, for her many contributions and ongoing encouragement.

BOOKS REFERENCED

BACKGROUND

Managing Retirement by Howard Shank, Contemporary Publishing, 1990

The Hero's Farewell by Jeffrey Sonnenfeld, Oxford University Press USA, 1991

The Organization Man by William H. Whyte and Joseph Nocera, University of Pennsylvania Press, 2002

New Passages by Gail Sheehy, Ballantine Books, 1996

Jack: Straight from the Gut by Jack Welch and John A. Byrne, Warner Business Books, 2003

The Nature of Personal Reality by Jane Roberts, Amber-Allen Publishing, 1994

Necessary Losses by Judith Vorst, Free Press, 1998

The Coming Age by Simone de Beauvoir, W.W. Norton & Company, 1996

A PLEASURABLE LIFE

Younger Next Year by Chris Crowley and Henry S. Lodge, Workmen Publishing Company, 2004

Aging Well by George E. Vaillant, Little, Brown and Company, 2003

A FULFILLING LIFE

Authentic Happiness by Martin Seligman, Ph.D., Free Press, 2004

For Men Only and *For Women Only* by Jeff Feldhahn and Shaunti Feldhahn, Multnomah, 2006

The Five Love Languages by Gary Chapman, North Field Publishing 1995

A GRATIFYING LIFE

The Power of Positive Thinking by Norman Vincent Peale, Ballantine Books, 1996

The Purpose-driven Life by Rick Warren, Zondervan, 2002

A MEANINGFUL LIFE

Man's Search For Meaning by Viktor E. Frankl, Pocket, 1997

The Power of Intention by Wayne W. Dyer, Hay House, 2005

Healthy Aging by Andrew Weil, M. D., Knopf, 2005

ABOUT THE AUTHOR

Douglas S. Fletcher, a management consultant and founding partner of Performex, has helped thousands of upper-level executives gain the edge in their management and leadership skills. For the past twenty-five years, his performance-management methods have been implemented in numerous Fortune 500 firms as taught through countless management seminars and workshops.

Now he has turned his attention to helping people apply similar skills in retirement. His *Life After Work* seminars, based on the book, have been hailed by hundreds of retirees. He has published two other books, *Understanding Organization Evolution: Its Impact on Management and Performance* (2002) and *Management Control in Today's Teamwork Organization: How to Get Things Done Without Exercising Direct Authority* (1991).

Fletcher holds a master's degree in business administration from The University of Chicago and a bachelor's degree in social psychology from UCLA.

For upcoming events, books, and videos of Fletcher's seminars visit his web site: http://lifeafterfulltimework.com.

CPSIA information can be obtained at www.ICGtesting.com
Printed in the USA
LVOW111939030212

266906LV00002B/232/A